"As a longtime personal injury lawyer and advocate for innovation in legal tech and AI, I've seen Seth Price lead the way in helping firms thrive online. His work with BluShark Digital has set a new standard—and this book is a masterclass in how he does it."

—MICHAEL McCREADY

Founder, McCready Law

"Seth Price is one of the great minds in our industry and an expert on SEO. Doing SEO well is critical for law firms. Do not miss out on these vital lessons from Seth, which are sure to drive more effective SEO for your firm!"

—JOHN NACHAZEL

COO, Mike Morse Law Firm

"When Seth asked me if I would write a snippet in support of a book he was writing, I said yes, not even knowing what the book was about. You see, Seth has been a friend and mentor to me for many years. He has been nothing but kind in an industry that sometimes can be harsh. He has made business and personal suggestions to me that have turned into gold. In short, he is a good human.

Now I know his topic (I really knew it all the time) and the book is full of the same gold he helped me spin. He can do it for you too. Read, pay attention, and learn ... good stuff right here!"

—TIM McKEY

Owner and CEO, Vista Consulting, Inc.

"A 'Must-Read Masterclass in Digital Domination for Law Firms.' Seth Price, Esq.'s book is a game-changing blueprint for lawyers and law firm owners looking to harness the explosive power of digital marketing. Blending hard-earned experience with crystal-clear instruction, Price breaks down the art and science of SEO—from content strategy to local search dominance—into an accessible, actionable guide. Price's journey from scrappy startup to powerhouse firm, fueled by fearless experimentation and a belief in the internet's untapped potential, offers not just inspiration, but a practical roadmap for any attorney ready to scale. Whether you're a solo practitioner or managing a regional practice, this is the book that will take your online presence—and your client intake—to the next level."

—JOHN FISHER

Owner and Founder, John H. Fisher, P.C. and Fisher Mastermind

"I have used the concepts of the Pareto Principle in managing law firms with great success, and now Seth has applied it to the world of legal marketing. This book shows you how to focus on the 20 percent of your efforts that generate 80 percent of your cases. It is a must-read for anyone in our industry. It will help you zero in on the strategies that work, and say no to all the noise that gets in the way."

—CHAD DUDLEY

Managing Partner, Dudley DeBosier Injury Lawyers

"Seth Price's expertise in local search is a game changer for law firms. In this book, he brilliantly combines cutting-edge local SEO strategies with proven techniques for handling large-scale litigation, offering invaluable insights to attorneys who want to dominate both their local markets and the mass tort arena. A must-read for any firm looking to grow and thrive in today's competitive legal landscape."

—MIKE PAPANTONIO

Managing Partner, Levin Papantonio

"Seth Price is a rare force in our industry—someone who's built both a top-performing law firm and one of the most respected digital marketing agencies in the country. That dual perspective—part practitioner, part strategist—is what makes his book on local search so powerful. It's not a theory. It's a tactical playbook built from real-world experience on both sides of the table."

—JENNIFER GORE-CUTHBERT

Partner, Sweet James Law Firm

"I live in a world of phone numbers but believe in all aspects of marketing. Seth has shown me that marketing success can come from local search as well. Not as well as phone numbers, mind you, but it works pretty darn well."

—COOL GUY PAUL (FAUST)

(Paul doesn't believe in titles.)

"Seth Price isn't just the founder of a multi-state law firm and the CEO of BluShark Digital—he's the real deal. He's the guy who shows up for his friends, who listens, who gives you honest, grown-up advice when you need it most. When Seth decided to write a book on local search, I couldn't think of anyone better. Why? Because he approaches this topic the same way he approaches everything in life—with candor, integrity, and a relentless commitment to results."

—BILL UMANSKY

Founder, The Umansky Law Firm

"I've spent years trying to wrap my head around SEO, and this is the first time it actually made sense. The way everything is broken down feels clear and doable, even if you're not a marketing expert. It's tailored specifically for law firms, which makes all the difference. If you're tired of generic advice, this book is a game changer."

—BEN GLASS

Founder, Ben Glass Law

"The mystery of SEO—the blend of science, art, and judgment—often leads business owners to stifle their own growth. Now, we have the tool to overcome our own inertia. The concepts in this book are genuinely accessible, including for those without a marketing background. Price's guidance is built around the realities of running a law practice, making it a true breakthrough. SEO can actually make sense—and now it does."

—ALLISON WILLIAMS

Founder, Law Firm Mentor

"If you run a law firm or manage marketing in a competitive space, this book is a game changer. Seth built a digital strategy that not only works but scales. I've seen it with my own eyes as he took our firm from worst to first in one of the largest markets in America and he's grown his own business using these exact principles. No guesswork, just proven tactics and a thoughtful approach that respects your budget and your brand. He understands how high the stakes are, and it shows in every chapter. Bottom line, I trust Seth to lead us into the digital frontier and you can, too."

—BILL BIGGS

Executive Director, Garces, Grabler, Lebrocq

"A masterclass in modern legal marketing. This insightful guide by a trailblazing attorney in SEO is a must-read for any lawyer—whether just starting out or seasoned in the field—who wants to attract clients and grow their practice."

—ANDREW FINKELSTEIN

Managing Partner, Finkelstein & Partners, LLP

"Seth's advice is to be followed—full stop. I have coaching clients who work with BluShark Digital and get fantastic results. Now lawyers can get his playbook to learn from one of the best. Law firm owners, you must get this book!"

—CHARLEY MANN

Founder, Law Firm Alchemy

"Seth brings a wealth of knowledge and experience to the table. His insights into legal marketing are both practical and forward-thinking, making this book an essential read for any law firm looking to enhance their online presence and attract more clients."

—KEITH GIVENS

Managing Shareholder, The Cochran Firm

"With all of the recent upheavals in the digital marketing space, this is the book every law firm owner needs to read. This book is the essential primer for law firm owners who want to understand the strategies behind the services they are buying and the vendors they are hiring. Seth's mastery of local SEO and insights into where digital marketing is headed make this book a must-read for any law firm owner serious about scaling."

—TOM TONA

Founder, Tona Law

"There aren't many in legal marketing as respected and knowledgeable as Seth Price. As both a law firm owner and founder of a top-tier SEO agency, he delivers real results and truly cares about helping firms grow. What sets him apart is how he makes something as complex as digital marketing feel clear, actionable, and even exciting. When firms implement his strategies, the impact is obvious: more qualified leads, better visibility, and more signed cases. If you're in the legal space and want to finally make SEO work, this book is for you."

—GARY FALKOWITZ

Founder, Law Firm Intake Guru

"I've known Seth long enough to say this, he doesn't gatekeep what he knows. This book is the perfect example of that. It's honest, straightforward, and full of lessons learned the hard way. You can tell it was written by someone who's actually been in the trenches, not someone selling theory. It feels like you're getting the kind of advice a friend would give you if they genuinely wanted to see you win. And that's exactly who Seth is."

—KEN HARDISON

Founder, PILMMA

"Finally—a clear, concise guide to mastering SEO. Seth Price doesn't just explain the theory; he provides an actionable roadmap packed with tools and strategies that enable lawyers to dominate their market online. I highly recommend every lawyer read this book!"

—KRISTEN DAVID

Founder, Upleveling Your Business

LOCAL SEO FOR LAWYERS

HOW ATTORNEYS CAN RANK HIGHER,
GET FOUND FASTER, AND GROW SMARTER

LOCAL
SEO
FOR
LAWYERS

SETH PRICE
AND DAVID BRENTON

Advantage | Books

Published by Advantage Books, Charleston, South Carolina.
An imprint of Advantage Media.

ADVANTAGE is a registered trademark, and the Advantage colophon is a trademark of Advantage Media Group, Inc.

Printed in the United States of America.

10 9 8 7 6 5 4 3 2 1

ISBN: 978-1-64225-737-3 (Hardcover)
ISBN: 978-1-64225-736-6 (eBook)

Library of Congress Control Number: 2025926986

Cover design by Lance Buckley.
Layout design by Megan Elger.

This publication is designed to provide accurate and authoritative information in regard to the subject matter covered. It is sold with the understanding that the publisher is not engaged in rendering legal, accounting, or other professional services. If legal advice or other expert assistance is required, the services of a competent professional person should be sought.

Advantage Books is an imprint of Advantage Media Group. Advantage Media helps busy entrepreneurs, CEOs, and leaders write and publish a book to grow their business and become the authority in their field. Advantage authors comprise an exclusive community of industry professionals, idea-makers, and thought leaders. For more information go to **advantagemedia.com**.

CONTENTS

INTRODUCTION 1

CHAPTER 1 7
GOOGLE 101

CHAPTER 2 21
**THE FUNDAMENTALS OF LINKS
AND OFF-PAGE SEO**

CHAPTER 3 35
HOW TO CREATE A LINK-BUILDING STRATEGY

CHAPTER 4 51
CONTENT IS STILL KING

CHAPTER 5 63
THE KEY TO KEYWORDS

CHAPTER 6 71
OPTIMIZE YOUR WEBSITE CONTENT

CHAPTER 7 85
IF IT'S NOT INDEXED, IT DOESN'T EXIST

CHAPTER 8 101
STRUCTURE TO WIN

CHAPTER 9 113
**HOW TO RANK, EXPAND, AND
DOMINATE LOCAL SEARCH**

CHAPTER 10 129
THE SCIENCE OF PAID SEARCH

CHAPTER 11 143
LANDING CLIENTS, NOT JUST CLICKS

CHAPTER 12 155
LSAS AND THE FUTURE OF PAID SEARCH

CONCLUSION 169
TWO STEPS YOU CAN TAKE TODAY

ABOUT THE AUTHOR. 179

INTRODUCTION

n the early 2000s, the dot-com bubble was bursting. Investors were rapidly losing faith in the internet and the products being sold online. The pivotal question of how the internet would shape the modern economy remained uncertain.

People recognized the internet's potential to provide information, yet its broader applications, particularly in commerce and business growth, were still largely unexplored. Businesses had yet to dedicate budgets specifically to digital marketing, and search engine optimization (SEO)—now a cornerstone of digital marketing—was barely in its infancy.

At that exact time, my law partner David Benowitz and I were navigating our own challenges, seeking ways to launch our fledgling law firm. Having successfully established our first practice in Washington, DC, we were ambitious and excited, expanding by hiring attorneys in Maryland and Virginia and eagerly discussing future practice groups and support staff additions. Yet, despite our growth, we faced the critical issue of having lawyers but needing cases.

Believing deeply in the internet's future potential, we decided to test a then-unconventional idea and launched our first website focused on driving under the influence (DUI) in Washington, DC. It was dreadful. The design was rudimentary, the content was awkwardly stuffed with keywords, and the backlinks pointing to our site came predominantly from the Philippines.

Surprisingly, none of these glaring imperfections mattered because it worked spectacularly. Our phones began ringing nonstop with people urgently needing assistance in their DUI cases. Encouraged by this initial success, we quickly launched two more websites targeting Maryland and Virginia.

We never anticipated that our humble beginning would lead us to where we stand today, operating more than twenty-five websites, employing lawyers across five states, managing over thirty office locations, and establishing an unmatched digital presence within our market. Witnessing firsthand the transformative power of digital marketing, we realized that our firm's remarkable growth was built fundamentally on leveraging online strategies. Recognizing the immense potential, we soon assembled an in-house team dedicated to optimizing our websites, strategically launching new office locations, and maximizing the conversions driven by our expanding web traffic. Our initial team, comprising a content editor, a link builder, a web development expert, and a local SEO specialist, became the foundation of our now comprehensive SEO strategy.

Initially born from our internal marketing department and shaped from the ground up as an agency built by lawyers—specifically for lawyers—this dedicated team would later evolve into BluShark Digital. We envisioned BluShark as more than just another marketing vendor; it was to be a genuine partner in law firm growth. At its core, BluShark's philosophy remained grounded in the fundamental principles of successful SEO: a robust technical foundation, extensive libraries of high-quality original content, authoritative backlinks, and a strong, strategic emphasis on local search. These four components are critical; omit even one, and maximizing your return on investment (ROI) from digital marketing becomes a challenge.

Today, BluShark Digital stands as a dominant force in legal digital marketing, employing a team of more than one hundred professionals who live and breathe SEO. Specialists meticulously focus on each core area—technical SEO, content creation, backlink building, and local SEO—to ensure our clients achieve measurable, sustainable success.

In this book, we will provide you with a comprehensive road map for launching a powerful SEO campaign, arming you with the knowledge to identify optimal keywords, craft compelling content, and implement the best on-page SEO practices. We will empower you with foundational development strategies to ensure your digital presence is built on a solid foundation, discuss the critical impact of local search, and share strategies to enhance your local rankings significantly. Ultimately, we will demonstrate precisely why SEO is indispensable—it's the fuel igniting growth within your law firm.

Reflecting on our beginnings nearly two decades ago, David and I started Price Benowitz LLP from the basement of his home in DC, strictly as a criminal defense practice with just the two of us—David as the lawyer and me as the marketing force. Starting from scratch, we created our first website, gradually hired more attorneys, launched additional sites, and methodically grew the firm. Fast-forward to today, and Price Benowitz LLP is unrecognizable from those humble origins. We now boast over 50 attorneys and more than 120 support staff across multiple practice areas.

One humorous anecdote from our early days involved hiring an intern, also named David (David Brenton), whom, to avoid confusion, we simply called "Brenton." He has been my right-hand man in writing this book and is the "we" I'm referring to whenever I make that reference. Brenton quickly proved invaluable, rising from intern to head of marketing, eventually leading the creation of BluShark Digital over ten years ago.

BluShark's rapid evolution from a small internal team to an influential agency representing over three hundred clients nationwide underscores our unique expertise: mastering local search. While traditional SEO methods, such as content creation and authoritative link building, remain essential, strategically dominating local search results elevated our clients to unparalleled visibility and success.

With this book, my mission is to combine my personal journey and industry insights into an actionable guide, clearly illustrating how our strategic emphasis on local SEO transformed our modest basement operation into a thriving, multilocation firm—and how employing these same proven principles can empower your own business to achieve similar remarkable growth.

If you are reading this book, there is a high likelihood that you know what SEO is. It refers to the practice of optimizing your website for higher rankings in the search results. By ranking higher, there is a better chance that you will generate traffic to your website and, in turn, leads.

Search engine marketing (SEM) is how someone leverages all the different aspects of the search engine to market their business. As we will discuss, there are many components of a search engine, and you need a well-rounded strategy for each of these elements in order to be successful.

Many people ask me when they should start thinking about SEO, and I always say, "Right now." There is no easy or right time to start running SEO campaigns. If you want to generate leads from the internet or if you care about your online brand reputation, you should have an SEO strategy in place. The legal industry is one of the most competitive industries for SEO.

For example, "mesothelioma lawyer" remains one of the most expensive clicks in the world, and other legal phrases round out the list of the top ten most expensive SEO terms. That is why you need to start now. If you are not thinking about SEO, I assure you that your competitors are, so there is no better time than now to start SEO for your website.

SEO is so much more than just a marketing tool—it's the foundation for sustainable growth in today's legal space. In this book, you'll find the same road map that helped us scale: a balanced focus on technical strength, original content, authoritative links, and local search. With the right strategy, your firm can achieve the growth you need in this increasingly digital world.

CHAPTER 1

GOOGLE 101

When I first met American hip-hop artist Flavor Flav, I'd recently left the secure world of Big Law for the unpredictable thrill of the late-1990s dot-com boom. I was at a trade show pitching my startup, EZCD.com, a website that let users create their own customized music compilation CDs. At the time, this felt revolutionary—remember, this was before iTunes and Spotify—but Flavor Flav didn't seem particularly impressed by CDs or my detailed plans to license his music.

Realizing I needed something fresh to capture his attention, I decided to quickly pivot to another idea. I introduced Flavor Flav to something completely new—a simple, fast, and seemingly magical way to find information online called "Google." Google was brand new at the time, an innovative search engine that made finding accurate information incredibly easy. And so, there we were: Flavor Flav, Big Mac in one hand, leaned over my keyboard to run his first ever Google search.

While we may not have realized it in that moment, the internet was here, ready to reshape how we find and interact with information.

That shift would soon extend to more traditional industries, including the one I'd recently left.

Back then, most lawyers wouldn't touch the internet. Trying to persuade attorneys of the value of an online presence felt like pulling teeth. However, over twenty-five years later, things have undergone a complete transformation. Now, lawyers at all levels, from solo practitioners to giant law firms with thousands of attorneys, recognize the importance of tools such as search engine optimization (SEO) and digital advertising. These online strategies have become essential to building credibility, attracting new clients, and sustaining successful businesses.

What hasn't changed, though, is the critical importance of curiosity and adaptability. Whether it was introducing Flavor Flav to Google decades ago or convincing skeptical lawyers to take their practices online, success has always depended on our willingness to explore new opportunities and technologies. Ultimately, lasting success comes from staying curious, learning continuously, and having the courage to chase after future trends. In hockey terms, it means skating toward where the puck is going rather than where it is in the current moment.

Common Misconceptions

We have all experienced it. We wake up, check our email, and find thousands of emails to go through. Buried in those emails is one from Deepak. Deepak promises you first-page rankings within a week of signing up for his SEO campaign. He guarantees that he can rank you for your main keywords, "car accident lawyer," and promises all of his tactics are white hat. Deepak is full of shit.

Common misconceptions about SEO abound in the legal industry. Because it is so competitive and costly, we know agencies will say just about anything to get you to sign up with them. There are no guarantees in SEO. All we have are historical data and a strategy that we think is going to be successful. Until we deploy that strategy and see how Google reacts, it is impossible to guarantee first-page rankings or the performance of a given web page. If you are on a sales pitch, and the salesperson guarantees you results, run.

Another common misconception about SEO is that you can rank things quickly. This is when you make a change to your website and Google understands it right away and reacts to it. That is absolutely not the case. SEO campaigns take time to see results.

Typically, our BluShark clients see an increase in results at launch, an even larger jump six to twelve months into their campaign, and a massive jump in months twenty-four to twenty-six. Part of the reason for this is that Google needs time to understand a business and its website. It needs time to understand the SEO strategy that you are implementing, and it needs time to get familiar and comfortable with you. Further, we know user signals, such as click-through rates from the search engine results page (SERP), are an important ranking factor. The more traffic you get to a site that is healthy, the more user signals Google has to determine how good an experience that user had on your site. SEO takes time; anyone who says they can rank you in a week is not telling you the full truth.

Some sketchy SEO agencies will deploy black-hat tactics to achieve quicker results. Usually, these tactics involve building exact-match anchor text links back to the domain they are working on. We will discuss this practice in greater detail later on; however, it is extremely risky from an SEO standpoint and can put you in the SEO doghouse. As we discussed, SEO takes time, and backlink building in particular can be a cumbersome effort. Some of our BluShark link-building projects run for eight months or even a year. Because of this, shortcuts with link building are taken all the time and can result in serious long-term damage to your website and brand.

Google from Sixty Thousand Feet

Whenever I first start talking about Google, I always begin with the purpose of the search. Search engines were created to connect user queries with information. Search is the primary way to access that information, and Google processes billions of searches on a daily basis. Google is constantly crawling the internet and indexing the content on those websites.

The Google bot is a complex organism that relies on its data and instinct when deciding which websites to show at the top of its search results. This organism does not like to be confused or misled.

So, how do you capture its attention? How do you guide the search engine to an understanding of you and your business?

Throughout this book, we will discuss Google and search engines generally in this light. We will consider the different factors that make this organism tick, and we will come up with strategies you can deploy in your business to start rising to the top.

It wasn't always this difficult to rank on Google. Before, when the algorithm was more antiquated, including the keywords on your website, having your keywords in your domain name and building some backlinks from anywhere would move you to the first page of Google. But times have changed. The amount of information that the algorithm can process is at an all-time high, and Google is utilizing technology to interpret data that we have never seen before. It is more difficult and competitive than ever to rank on Google, especially in the legal space—so how do you go about doing it?

Don't worry—as promised, we will share our proven road map with all you need to achieve SEO success. Search engines rely on users to conduct searches. Without people searching them, search engines are gigantic, untapped databases of information. Google understands this and is constantly making tweaks to the search engine and SERP. It is important to understand the makeup of the SERP, especially as it has evolved over the years.

When I first started this business, the SERP comprised some paid ads at the top, seven listings on the local map, and ten organic listings on the first page of Google. Now, you have three Local Services Ads (LSAs) at the top of the page; three listings in the map pack, with usually one paid ads listing; and ten organic links on the home page, with some sponsored paid ads options showing above or below the map pack, depending on the search term. Up until July of 2024, Google had an endless scroll for search on mobile devices, meaning a user did not need to select the next page to view positions eleven to twenty.

Google continues to change the appearance of the SERP as a way to keep users coming back to Google. In addition, it is in Google's best interest to keep people on Google, and the SERP features it has released in the last ten years reflect that thinking. For example, the increase in rich snippet results, or results that show up larger and highlighted before anything else, as well as knowledge panels for certain terms, are but a few examples of how Google is launching products to keep people on the SERP. The team at Google is always asking, "How can we give users as much information as possible without them ever leaving the search engine?" This has to be a question that is at the forefront of the minds of those at Google, and when Google comes out with new products search engine marketers can utilize, these reflect this mentality.

Let's take a minute to reflect on all the information you can get from the SERP about a business without ever leaving Google. All of the business's demographic information is available on its Google Business Profile (GBP), along with customer reviews, frequently asked questions, and photos of your office. Google has the "People also ask" section on the SERP, which allows you to follow up your questions with additional queries. Further, you can check out videos of a business with a simple click, see how the business fares on third-party review sites, and discover if there is any recent press that has mentioned the company—all without leaving Google. Ultimately, Google gets paid when ads get clicked, so new SERP functions usually have an eye toward paid ads.

Google is not the only search engine out there. Bing, Duck-DuckGo, and others have begun to crop up, each with different incentives for searchers to use them. Some are advertising a more private search, while others, such as Bing, are integrating with artificial intelligence (AI). Google is the most used search engine by far, clocking in over 90 percent of overall search traffic.[1] That is why, for this book, our focus will be on Google. Understand that many of the SEO tactics we talk about, when deployed properly, will result in SEO success on these other search engines, but Google is really the gold standard of search.

One thing you should know about Google is that its teams work with relative independence from one another. The team that works on paid search is different from the local and organic teams. This is an important distinction because of how the search engine operates. The

---

1   Tiago Bianchi, "Market Share of Leading Search Engines Worldwide from January 2015 to March 2025," Statista, accessed June 23, 2025, https://www.statista.com/statistics/1381664/worldwide-all-devices-market-share-of-search-engines/.

local and organic algorithms, as we will discuss in great detail later, work independently from one another.

Further, purchasing paid traffic through Google Ads will not necessarily result in an increase in organic or local rankings. There is an argument to be made that paying for good, healthy traffic does improve your overall website quality in Google's eyes. However, there is no proof of this. For our purposes, the teams are entirely independent, and you should have a unique optimization strategy for each aspect of the search engine you plan to target.

Spam Comes in Many Forms

Further, Google cares a great deal about the integrity of the search results. If its search results are poor or are delivering results for shady businesses, its users will notice. A search engine, after all, is only as good as its results. If people are spamming the internet to manipulate those search results, it looks bad on Google. Google has gotten better and better at detecting web spam, but it is still pervasive throughout the internet. We are going to cover the basics of spam, what happens when you get caught, and how you should think about aggressive SEO techniques moving forward.

Spam comes in all shapes and sizes, but for our purposes, we will be focusing on three core types of spam: link spam, content spam, and technical spam. All three of these used to work, but as Google has gotten smarter and released algorithm updates to crack down on spam, their effect has become less and less powerful. Further, the risks of spamming can't be overstated. Google can and will penalize a website or web page that it feels is spamming the internet or compromising the integrity of the search results.

CONTENT SPAM

Content spam has reduced over the last eight years, but it still exists. Google has launched quite a few updates, most recently, the helpful content update, with an eye toward removing websites that are spamming content from the search results. Some examples of ways content spam has historically been used include spinning content (changing the order of words and reusing a page of content), spamming a page with keywords (including unnatural keywords in content way too much), or even outright plagiarizing and copying entire pages of content from other websites.

More advanced versions of content spam may use doorway or gateway pages to lure a victim into their grasp before striking with terrible content. Stay away from any and all of these methods of developing content. Your page won't rank, and you could end up in serious Google trouble.

LINK SPAM

Link spam has also reduced over the years through the deployment of updates and SEO practitioners generally cleaning up their acts and being more cautious with link building. Link building, or building backlinks to your site from another as a way to develop authority, has been a powerful tool for optimizing search results since its inception. However, spamming your website with links from low-authority sources that have no relevance to your business or are published on foreign-language blogs or forums is not a good idea.

Link spammers will purchase boatloads of links from places across the internet. From random blogs to forums about cars, these links can pop up anywhere. Further, many link spammers will spam the anchor text or literal words on the hyperlink with keywords that they want to be found for. The intention of a campaign like this is to build a large volume of links as quickly and cheaply as possible.

Google has launched a series of updates to catch link spammers. Now, the search bot is getting to such a sophisticated level that it can discount or skip links that it knows to be spammy. In other words, if the search bot crawls a link and wonders why it is there, it may just pass over it without crediting it to the linked site at all. Because of this, spammy link building has become slightly less risky, and it has also decreased the reward. However, Google takes link spam very seriously, and you should think twice before deploying any spammy links in your SEO campaign.

TECHNICAL SPAM

Another form of spam that may not appear as obvious is **technical spam**. Technical spam can take many forms, but at its face value, it involves manipulating the code of your website or aspects of the code to influence the search results. One example of this was someone who came to me with a penalty from Google for spamming their metadata. I had never seen anything like it before, but Google had issued them a penalty in Google Search Console for spamming their structured data with keywords.

Two Types of Penalties

ALGORITHMIC PENALTIES

If you do partake in some spammy activities, you should understand the risks. Google can and will issue penalties for manipulating the search results. These penalties come in two forms: manual actions and algorithmic penalties. Let's start with the less severe **algorithmic penalties**. These were typically issued after algorithm updates, although they don't have to be and would typically target a specific URL or page on your website instead of the entire domain.

Usually, this page would fall out of the search rankings, and traffic to it would stop until the penalty was lifted. It should be noted that Google will not tell you a web page has a penalty. You will have to deduce that something happened to that page when it falls in the rankings or traffic stops coming to it. Focus on the impacted page, as algorithmic penalties should not impact every page on the domain.

MANUAL ACTION PENALTIES

Manual action penalties can be more problematic. We will go into manual actions and the process for reconsideration reviews in greater detail later. However, it is worth noting that if you are issued a manual action penalty, it will impact your entire domain. You will get a notification in Google Search Console that a penalty has been issued, and your website will completely fall out of the SERP. You will need to go through a process with Google to show you are sorry for your errant ways and have made amends. This process is cumbersome, expensive, and takes forever. Keep this in mind whenever you are thinking about pushing spammy SEO tactics.

The Many Hats of SEO Specialists

BLACK-HAT SEO

You may be at your next SEO conference and hear the phrase *black hat*. What does that mean? Well, black-hat SEO practitioners are those who use spammy tactics to manipulate the search results. Usually, their tactics are not natural and do not add value to the internet as a whole.

GRAY-HAT SEO

Gray-hat SEO practitioners are individuals who understand the nuances of spam. They understand the importance of the different SEO elements and will try in the most natural way possible to manipulate the search results.

WHITE-HAT SEO

White-hat SEO practitioners are completely clean. They would not touch spam or a spammy tactic with a ten-foot pole. These individuals are more cautious with their tactics and will always be thinking about being natural in their content and links. These lines can get extremely blurry, especially when you are thinking of new creative ways to build links or develop content. Always try to stay grounded with what you know; Google wants webmasters to add value to the internet, improve their search results, and answer the questions their searchers are asking. If you are doing these things, you should be able to stay in Google's good graces.

Google Updates

Google has a rich history of releasing updates to its search engine algorithm. Up until 2019, Google would not publicly announce when it was releasing an update or when the rollout had been completed. Instead, search marketers were left to check their SEO data, keeping their ear to the ground in the SEO community and trying to predict when Google would be launching updates. Google has since done us the courtesy of announcing updates. These updates can take many forms, all of which we will discuss briefly.

The largest and most impactful type of update is a core algorithm update. When these updates occur, they typically involve the search engine changing or weighing differently the signals it picks up on during a crawl. These core updates are foundational to the algorithm and the factors that it considers when choosing to rank a site. Some examples of core updates include Google's Helpful Content Update in 2022, which penalized websites that focused on rankings rather than value to users; Google's Core Update in 2023 that prioritized useful and original content; and Google's Core Update in June 2025, which changed the way content, especially AI-generated content, is evaluated for relevance and user intent. Core updates have historically had the greatest impact on organic search, although by definition, they shake up the SERP.

The other type of algorithm update that Google will launch is more targeted updates. These usually specifically target some part of the algorithm that Google has identified that people are spamming. Some examples of targeted algorithm updates include Panda and Penguin. These updates specifically targeted content and link spam that were pervasive throughout the internet.

How do you determine if your website was impacted by a Google update? Well, like in the old days, you need to rely on your website and SEO metrics to tell you if there is a problem. You should be tracking your rankings on a weekly basis. If you start to notice that your rankings are dropping or fluctuating more than normal, something may be afoot.

Next, if your rankings drop, there is a decent chance your traffic dropped as well. Go into Google Analytics and sort your pages by traffic losses. This should correlate with your rankings losses and will help you pinpoint where you need to spend time optimizing. If your losses are in a specific practice area, figure out what the update was targeting and implement corrective measures on those practice area pages. Understanding how to adapt after a Google update is critical for SEO success because Google comes out with updates so frequently. Especially now, SEO practitioners need to be nimble and able to adapt their strategy based on the situation in front of them.

Keeping Up with Google

Every Google update is designed with the searcher in mind. Remember, Google needs people to trust the search results they are being provided with. If the integrity of the search results is compromised, it can lead to searchers going somewhere else for information, something Google absolutely cannot allow. That's why staying aligned with Google's priorities is crucial for a successful SEO strategy. In later chapters, we'll discuss how specific updates have impacted best practices in local SEO, content creation, and link building.

CHAPTER 2

THE FUNDAMENTALS OF LINKS AND OFF-PAGE SEO

After defending my first deposition ever, I turned to the opposing counsel—someone I had just spent hours jousting with—and casually asked if she'd like to check out the Field of Dreams.

It was my first year as an associate, and I'd go on to spend countless hours flying around the Midwest defending depositions. Early on, I made a personal rule: *Every* business trip should include something enjoyable beyond the legal work, whether that meant finding a great local restaurant, visiting a museum, or exploring a town's hidden gems.

The Field of Dreams, the iconic baseball diamond Kevin Costner built in a cornfield for the movie, was just thirty minutes away from our deposition location in Dyersville, Iowa. Despite our combative morning, my adversary surprisingly agreed. The drive changed everything.

Instead of opposing attorneys, we became just two young professionals sharing the journey, discussing our careers, aspirations, and uncertainties. That afternoon, adversaries became teammates, shagging fly balls, playing an impromptu baseball game, and even drawing a small crowd, thanks to a curious busload of German tourists.

That day taught me a fundamental truth: Beneath baseball's intricate strategies and complex tactics lies an elegant simplicity. Similarly, behind the intense competition and complexities of the courtroom are the basic, universal elements of humanity—trust, credibility, and connection.

SEO Strategy Basics

The same principle applies to SEO. Digital marketing, much like baseball or the courtroom, often feels complex and filled with advanced techniques. Yet, at its core, success in SEO comes down to mastering a few essential fundamentals. Among these, few are more critical than links and off-page SEO.

Just as baseball players perfect their swing, stance, and throw to achieve consistency, longevity, and excellence on the field, digital marketers must consistently refine their link-building and off-page strategies. These foundational elements, executed correctly, create credibility with search engines, build authority in your industry, and ultimately provide lasting online visibility. Without solid fundamentals, even the most advanced SEO tactics won't deliver sustainable results.

A core component of a strong SEO strategy is the implementation of an off-page SEO or link-building strategy. Off-page SEO refers to the use of optimization techniques that do not occur on your website in order to improve your ranking in the search results. The goal of any off-page SEO strategy is to increase the authority of the website to which you are attempting to build links.

The more your website is linked to, the more Google sees it as an authority, and this authority, or "link equity," is passed from the linking site to the linked site. The more authoritative the website you are getting the link from, the more authority will be passed to your website. Think of backlinks as endorsements that websites give each other across the internet. The more endorsements you get, the more Google will see you as an authority and move you up the search results.

Google is constantly crawling the internet and picking up on these endorsements, almost banking them in its database. The more of these endorsements that you bank over time, the more authoritative Google will see your website as being. Links do not necessarily stay up forever. As pages are deleted or moved around, or even as webmasters find a better and more relevant source, links are replaced or lost frequently. Link building is an extremely powerful lever an SEO specialist can pull when needed to move a page up the search results.

The power of link building can't be overstated. Backlinks are the fastest way to rank a website on the search engines. Simply writing more words than your competitor and including keywords in your page of content are not enough. In order for that page of content to rank, you must build its authority. Link building serves as the nexus between what is occurring on your website and what is occurring throughout the ether of the internet. Your goal with off-page SEO is to find and place your link on the most authoritative sources possible to pass equity and drive traffic.

In this chapter, we will discuss how to get started with off-page SEO. We will go over the basics of link building, how to track links during an off-page SEO strategy, and Google's troubled history with link building. Backlink creation is the number one thing that SEO practitioners wish they could spend more time on because of the power that off-page SEO has. Off-page SEO is not something that happens overnight. You need to have a well-developed plan that is implemented over a long period of time to see continued success. Further, it is not enough to build one link and leave it. You need to continually think of new cutting-edge ways to build backlinks to your site.

The History of Google and Off-Page SEO

Google has had a somewhat rocky relationship with link building, mostly because SEO practitioners take advantage of the power that link building holds and manipulate it to their advantage. Google has been forced to take steps to prevent or attempt to curtail the use of spammy link-building practices because they work. That being said, these practices come with some risk, so it is important to know the landscape before starting your link-building projects.

When the Penguin update was announced, it sent shock waves through the SEO industry. This update, launched by Google in 2012, was intended to address link spam that was pervasive across the internet. Websites were building links on other websites that were completely irrelevant to their business. They were spamming blogs with links, purchasing links in extremely obvious ways, farming links, posting links to their websites on random topical forums, commenting on other people's blogs with links to their websites, and overall, spamming the internet.

Google does forbid paying for links. Historically, some websites were link farms in the sense that they had a button in the top banner that said, "Get listed, pay now." There was no more obvious signal to Google that a link was paid for. Further, as we discuss later in this chapter, anchor text spam was targeted during this update. Lawyers were big perpetrators of link spam. When an area, such as legal, is hypercompetitive, it leads people to make questionable decisions. Shortcuts in link building led to serious issues, and we are about to learn all about them.

Penguin came through like a hurricane. What it did was change the algorithm so that it assumed that high-quality websites link to other high-quality websites and low-quality websites link to low-quality websites—so if you had low-quality links, your website was potentially low quality. Penguin specifically targeted link spam and had major SERP ramifications.

One of the things that came out of the Penguin update was the use of manual action penalties for link spam. These penalties, issued by Google, were extremely damaging to a business if it received one. Google would communicate manual action penalties to webmasters through Google Search Console. There, it would highlight some instances where link spam had been caught on the webmaster's domain.

A webmaster had the opportunity to submit a reconsideration review to Google, in which it would look through the changes the webmaster had made to their backlink profile and determine if they were out of the doghouse. While this process was playing out, the website would not appear in the search engine. Let me repeat that: If you received a penalty, your website would be ripped out of the search results and de-indexed until the penalty was lifted.

The reconsideration review process could take months to complete. This was not something that you or your agency could handle overnight. Google required you to find all the spammy links that were pointing to your website. You would then need to reach out to all those website providers and request that the links be taken down.

Some of these websites, which were already quite nefarious, would require a ransom to take the link down or would not respond at all. In order for the penalty to be lifted, Google would ask you to report the communication you had had with these webmasters, show everything you had done to try to get the penalty lifted (including paying any consultants), and if you were unsuccessful in getting the link removed, take the last resort of disavowing the link altogether.

One Google feature that came from this update was the disavow tool. As mentioned previously, you are not able to take down some links. The webmaster may have taken on other projects and may no longer be monitoring the website from which you were linked. Google understood this, and so it created the disavow tool as a way for webmasters to communicate to the search engine, "We know these links exist, we know that they are not good quality, so please do not pay attention to them and do not penalize us for them." The disavow tool required a file to be submitted in a specific format so that Google could read and understand it. When this tool was first introduced, some SEO practitioners had processes that would require them to manually update their disavow file every month.

It should be noted that the disavow tool has become less and less relevant. Some would even argue today that it has become essentially obsolete. As the algorithm evolved, it got much better at understanding the links it was crawling—in other words, systematically scanning and analyzing web pages to index their content and metadata. It has been able to associate links with websites in ways that seemed impossible before. Now, the search engine can crawl a link and almost instantly decide whether that link should pass equity to the linking site.

The search engine can evaluate and discount link spam during its crawl. In other words, if it passes over a link it doesn't like, it discredits it and moves on. Penalties have become much fewer and farther between. In fact, I have not personally seen a manual action penalty in over six years. This does not mean that you should revert to the ways of 2011 and start spamming the internet, but it does mean that every off-page action you take is being evaluated by Google. I would not recommend that you have a process for continuing to disavow links unless you are under attack from a competitor and have a black-hat link portfolio.

I was part of a mastermind group when Penguin was released, and a significant topic of discussion in that group was a concept called negative SEO. In the group, a personal injury (PI) lawyer had noticed his backlinks were going up by thousands per day from completely random and cringeworthy sources. We are talking about the worst of the worst sites, such as porn, gambling, and dark web–type backlinks.

The fact is, all of these, now over ten thousand unique links, were actually improving his rankings. He was seeing massive spikes in rankings and traffic across the state because of these links. After further investigation, it appeared that his competitor was the one building these links in an attempt to get Google to issue a penalty for his website. This tactic, known as negative SEO, emerged significantly after the Penguin update. Since Google was levying penalties, people thought they could get it to penalize their competitors. In some instances, it worked; in others, it did not. In this instance, the lawyer continued to disavow the bad links as they were built. However, Google continued to reward them with better rankings. This may be a one-off, but it illustrates the different ways SEO can be used for or against you.

Penguin's impact on SEO can't be overstated. Generally, SEO practitioners became more cautious about where they were building links. They became more intentional about the neighborhoods they wanted their website to be found in. There was almost a spaghetti-at-the-wall mentality before Penguin. The idea was to get as many links as possible, and it didn't matter where they were from. Penguin changed that for the better. It made sure that people were thinking about the links they were building. It made spamming the internet harder, which, overall, makes the internet a more fruitful environment, and it made link building much more difficult and more expensive.

Google has continued to release link spam updates since Penguin. These typically target a specific aspect of link building and have not looked as much at the overarching link portfolio that a business may have. Newer updates specifically targeted link spam or other off-page SEO tactics, such as redirecting expired domains into your domain to pass all the old link equity to the new site or crackdowns on larger private blog networks (PBNs).

To stay safe with Google, it is important to keep a watchful eye on your backlink portfolio and constantly evaluate where you are placing your links. Further, it is important to track the different types of links you are getting and where you are getting them from and to attempt to make sure you have as diverse a backlink portfolio as possible.

The Basics of Link Building

As we discussed, the goal with backlinks is to build your website's authority. However, not all websites are created equal, and this is also true for backlinks. So, how do you go about evaluating a website and determining if it is a worthy place to get a link? How do you know if the links you are building are actually improving the authority of your website? There are some metrics that a few tools give us that shed light on the overall status of your link-building campaigns.

Domain rating (DR) is a metric that tells us how authoritative a domain is. This is not a score that Google has or keeps. This is a metric provided by Ahrefs, an SEO tool that gives you data about how powerful a website is from an SEO perspective. The DR is a rough cumulative calculation of a number of different factors, including the authority of the links pointing to your website. DR alone should not be the only reason you choose whether or not to pursue a link. However, it does provide you with information about whether, overall, this is a neighborhood you want to be found in.

If the DR of a website is low (zero to ten), that means that the equity that is passed from that website will be nominal. Further, if it is not topical, then what is the point of pursuing a low-quality link on a website like this? This is not to say that your link portfolio should have no links of this nature, but rather, DR should be a component of your formula when determining how much effort to put behind a specific link-building effort.

URL rating (UR) is another metric that was developed by Ahrefs that measures the strength of a backlink profile for a specific page. It is calculated using a logarithmic scale from zero to one hundred, with a higher number indicating a higher quality and more authoritative backlink profile. The main difference between UR and DR is that UR measures a specific URL, whereas DR measures the domain overall.

When running a link-building campaign, you may be attempting to increase the rankings for specific keywords, such as "child custody lawyer." In this example, the URL you would be building links to is xyz.com/child-custody-lawyer. If you enter this URL specifically into Ahrefs, you will get a UR for it. When you run a link-building campaign to that URL, the UR should increase as more links are built to it.

Trust Flow (TF) is a metric developed by Majestic and is another tool that measures a website's perceived trustworthiness based on the quality and reputation of the website's backlinks. In other words, TF measures how influential a URL might be based on the quality and authority of the links pointing to it. TF was a way for SEO practitioners to measure link quality and evaluate whether a website was trustworthy enough to have a link on. While not the be-all-or-end-all metric, TF can be considered when evaluating how beneficial a link may be for your website.

You may be thinking, *Well, I don't want to go out and buy a bunch of SEO programs for my link-building campaign. How can I evaluate potential link-building opportunities myself?* The first thing to consider is always whether it makes sense for you to be listed there. Is the website that your link would be coming from topical or relevant to you or your business? If the answer to that question is no, it may be best to consider other opportunities.

Next, ask yourself if your link is naturally in the text of the page or if it is artificially inserted for the sake of adding a link. If a link can be naturally placed in the text and adds value to the user experience, it is most likely a good location. If the website is about party buses, and randomly, on a booking page, it says "DC accident lawyer" and is hyperlinked, that is not natural. The link should add value to the internet and provide an additional opportunity for the user to learn more about a particular topic.

Finally, evaluate the source of the link. What is this website? What is the purpose of the website? Is it relevant to your business, or is it a stretch? Understanding the website you are asking to be linked from is critical for link-building success.

Another important element of off-page SEO to consider is having a diverse backlink portfolio. What I mean by that is having a number of links coming from several different sources. These sources are referred to as "referring domains."

Referring domains are the separate domains that are linking to you. It is not enough to have twenty thousand links coming from one referring domain. That is the opposite of a diverse link portfolio, and you will not see success. Instead, it is much more valuable to have two hundred links from a hundred different sources. That diversity of sources, or diversity of referring domains, shows the search engine that you are a well-rounded website that gets endorsements from a wide variety of sources.

Further, think about it like a political campaign. Is it better for the candidate to get one endorsement shouted by the same person over and over again or one hundred different people saying different nice things about the candidate? The same is true for backlink diversity and backlink profiles overall. Think about all the different applicable sources from which you could get links. These include news sites, government websites, local business websites, local business profiles, national profiles (e.g., the Better Business Bureau or the Chamber of Commerce), university websites, and so on.

The more you can diversify where you are getting your links from, the more you show Google that you appeal to a wide audience of individuals. Typically, an agency will have a plan to target each of these website types and will launch projects to achieve those ends. A strong link-building proposal will include a plan to garner links from a wide variety of sources in a multitude of ways.

> The more you can diversify where you are getting your links from, the more you show Google that you appeal to a wide audience of individuals.

Nofollow Versus Dofollow Links

Another common question people ask me is how much they should pay attention to nofollow and dofollow links. Taking a step back, I first ask them if they know what these two words mean. Nofollow links are hyperlinks that tell a search engine not to pass authority or equity to the linked site. Think of nofollow links like soft endorsements. They are there, but the website linking to you is not 100 percent certain if they want to pass equity your way. Nofollow links are identified in the source code with the following code: <a rel="nofollow">.

Dofollow links tell the search engine to credit authority to the linking site. These links are identified in the source code as well, and a webmaster will determine which classification to assign to a link when they add it to their website. It is important to understand that nofollow links are still crawled and do provide value. They are typically easier to get and contribute to the overall diversity of your backlink portfolio. Dofollow links are the gold standard for link building. The more dofollow links from authoritative sources that you can get, the more likely your website is to rank and perform well for all the search terms you want to be found for.

People often ask me if social media shares, likes, or comments pass equity in the same way as link building. After all, a social share is an endorsement of sorts by a member of the general public or, sometimes, from a business or organization. The short answer to this question is no. Social shares do not pass equity to a website like link building does. Social media shares may help drive website traffic, which, in turn, will help to increase rankings, but generally speaking, they do not equate to authority. Further, if someone comes to you and says they have a great link-building strategy that involves a social influencer, you should probably run for the hills. Unless that influencer is a link-building influencer with access to hundreds of websites on which to build links (that are not considered a PBN), that is not a good use of your time or money.

Anchor text refers to the literal words used on the hyperlink linking to your website. Anchor text tells the search engine and the user, in a few short words, what the page they are about to click through to is about. The practice of using keywords as your anchor text has been around for quite some time. It is well documented and proven that having links with anchor text that you want to be found for helps move rankings for specific keywords.

In other words, if my rankings for "truck accident lawyer" were suffering, going out and building ten links with the words "truck accident lawyer" hyperlinked to my truck accident lawyer page would make an impact in moving those rankings up. However, anchor text needs to be used sparingly. As mentioned briefly earlier, the Penguin update targeted link spam that had spammy anchor text. It is not natural for a reader to come across the exact words of a Washington, DC, criminal defense attorney on a news site in the middle of an article about a local crack house bust.

When you are building links, it is important to consider the diversity of your anchor text. You do not always need to avoid exact-match anchor text for keywords. In fact, if there is a natural opportunity to use exact-match anchor text, we encourage you to do so. However, we all know that our keywords, at least as they are searched right now, do not sound natural.

Consider using your brand name as anchor text, or replace the word *lawyer* with *case* or *cases*. Both of these techniques soften the anchor text slightly from being an exact match to something that is relevant, topical, and more natural. Because of this, it is important to consider the context and literal words used during your link-building efforts.

Link building is a difficult and time-consuming process. You need a long-term strategy that encompasses a variety of links from a number of different sources when you are optimizing for off-page SEO. Further link-building practices are evolving every year, and Google is getting better at understanding off-page website signals. Remember to build links that are natural and add value to the internet, and keep an eye on your off-page SEO signals, such as DR, UR, and TF, to ensure your link-building strategy is on track.

Building Links to Build Trust

If you want to ensure the success of your off-page strategy, focus on quality and relevant backlinks, and avoid shortcuts that can lead to penalties. Google prioritizes natural, diverse link profiles, so building links will take time, patience, and a comprehensive plan. Keep in mind that SEO is about more than just rankings; it's also about establishing trust and authority over time.

CHAPTER 3

HOW TO CREATE A LINK-BUILDING STRATEGY

A s law firm owners and business leaders, we're constantly pulled in multiple directions. Client cases, billing, operations, marketing—you name it. Managing all these responsibilities effectively can be overwhelming, which is why many firms decide to hire a law firm administrator. But finding and fully leveraging this crucial hire comes with its own set of challenges.

The first challenge is finding the right fit. You need someone who not only grasps the unique complexities of a law firm but also brings the perfect mix of legal know-how, managerial talent, and cultural alignment. It's critical to find someone capable of balancing both the technical details and managing people effectively.

Second, clearly defining the role is crucial. Too often, confusion arises about what the administrator's role truly entails. Are they handling HR, accounting, office management, or all of the above? A lack of clarity leads to frustration.

The third challenge involves delegating responsibilities effectively. Law firm owners often find it difficult to hand off key tasks because relinquishing control, especially when the firm is your passion, isn't easy. Trusting your administrator's expertise and granting autonomy are harder than they seem.

Fourth is leveraging their full potential. Often, once hired, administrators are seen merely as administrative support rather than as strategic partners. The solution is to integrate them fully into your leadership team. Involve them in strategic discussions, client development, and improvement initiatives.

Finally, retaining and developing your administrator are vital. High turnover disrupts operations, so it's essential to engage and nurture this crucial role. Offer ongoing training and development opportunities, cultivate a culture of collaboration and respect, and ensure they feel valued as an integral member of your team.

Just as your firm thrives when it's structured around clearly defined roles and responsibilities, your digital strategy (especially your approach to link building) requires the same clarity and intentional design. Without a well-structured link-building strategy, your online presence can become chaotic and ineffective. In this chapter, we'll explore how to establish a robust, strategic approach to link building that mirrors the operational discipline successful firms employ.

Start with What You Have

Now that you have a basic understanding of off-page SEO, it is time to start developing a strategy to actually go out and get links. This may seem like a daunting task, but in reality, it just takes time and dedication. It takes a new mindset of always keeping an eye out for link opportunities and thinking up new creative ways to get people to link to your website.

The first thing I always tell people when coming up with a link-building strategy for the first time is to start with what they have. You may already have some mentions across the internet from past cases you did that were in the press. You may have given a testimonial for a friend's product or are listed as a board member of a local nonprofit you are involved with. All of these are fantastic and extremely easy places to get links. While the websites they are on may not be super authoritative, they are local and do tell Google a little about you and your business.

> Your goal in creating this strategy is to transfer your offline authority into link equity.

Next, scour the internet for past press mentions. Historically, press websites have been quite authoritative, which means getting a link from them can be very profitable for your business. Have someone on your team run Google searches with your last name and the last name of the individual whose case was mentioned in the press. If you are working with a public relations (PR) agency, make sure they know that one of the goals of your PR campaign is to link up any mentions of you or your brand. Even if the case was in the past, start calling and asking for links to be put up. You would be shocked at the results that you can get.

Your goal in creating this strategy is to transfer your offline authority into link equity. A great place to start is by thinking about your offline activity.

Where do you volunteer? Do you coach or teach? Do you speak at any conferences or events? Do you donate money regularly to a charity? All of these activities can be transferred to online link equity.

Steps to Take

First, write an impact piece on how that organization, activity, or opportunity made an impact in your life. *How did your life change? How do you carry yourself in your business?* In that piece, include a link and start making phone calls to those organizations, pitching the piece you wrote. You will be amazed at the response that you end up getting from these organizations. Many are happy to put up an impact piece such as this because it is genuine, and the organization wants to show that it or the activity truly made a difference in your life.

Another thing I always tell clients is to leverage the press or existing earned media of any partners or associates at the firm as well. Sometimes, firms have a partner who may have worked on a big case or may have an extremely active associate. You will have more success building links from existing offline or online relationships, so leverage those to the best of your ability to get quicker and easier links.

Further, you should leverage your other lawyers to build the volume of links you can get from certain sources. One easy link-building project you should deploy right now is professional profiles and directories. Historically, these legal directories, such as Avvo, Justia, and FindLaw, had greater authority, but the profiles that are on these properties do include an opportunity for you to link back to your website.

Some of them actually allow you to link to more than one page on your site, so keep this in mind when building out your profiles. If you have a law firm with ten lawyers, all of them should be listed in the directory, not only for the link opportunity but also for the potential lead generation that still exists on some of these directories in some markets. Further, look at bar association websites, professional memberships that have directories, or even some conferences that list speakers and attendees. Many things you do have professional directories tied to them, so keep this in mind when determining which dues to pay next.

Determine the Goal

When developing your link-building strategy, make sure to consider the sources of potential links and how you can diversify those sources.

One example of this is with .edu links. Educational links, or links coming from educational institutions, are notoriously difficult to get. Creating content that a university wants to link to is a tough task when the university itself is conducting countless research studies on a regular basis. Some law schools have alumni directories that you can take advantage of. I would highly recommend you look into this for your undergrad and graduate institutions, along with all your attorneys. If you can even get one or two links from this type of project, it is well worth it. We will discuss other specific avenues for achieving .edu links later in this chapter.

Now that we have leveraged our offline relationships, identified past press or online mentions, and explored professional and legal directories, we turn to link building through content or outreach. This form of link building is more cumbersome, costs more, and takes time to see results. However, if done right, you will be putting yourself ahead of your competition.

So, where do we start, and how do we come up with content that people want to link to?

The first thing you should do with any off-page SEO campaign is determine the goal of the campaign.

Where do I want to drive backlinks? Which page on my site? What would ideal anchor text look like? Next, you want to determine what type of outreach campaign this is. *Would people in my local market be interested in this? Would people be interested nationally, and if so, why?*

Once you have your answers to these questions, you can start to develop a list of what types of people may find the content for a specific campaign intriguing. *What types of organizations would find this interesting? More importantly, whose users would find whatever I am pitching to be of interest?* Once you have your ideal outreach avatar created, build your list. Develop your content and start making phone calls. Let's put this into action with a few project examples.

> 📌 Where do I want to drive backlinks? Which page on my site? What would ideal anchor text look like?

Create Resource Libraries

One way for you to generate backlinks to your site is by creating resource libraries that people actually want to link to. This may sound crazy, but the vast majority of people on the internet are looking for information. Providing useful information for users and other businesses will result in those users or businesses sharing the resource.

Many people who find an excellent resource want to tell the world about it. If you have a resource that people want to learn more about or visit, there is a decent chance that this will result in a link-building opportunity. Resource libraries, when done right, are a fantastic way for you to conduct outreach or naturally build links.

I came across a truly wonderful resource library on a website dedicated to college student defense. It had everything in there, from all the local institutions' codes of conduct, their policies for hearings (both academic and otherwise), resources for parents whose children were facing charges, etc. This resource library was a one-stop shop for all students in the state to use whenever they needed it. It was featured by local news outlets and shared across their websites.

Furthermore, the schools themselves started to link to this resource library, which provided some extremely valuable .edu links to the property. This eventually led to even greater success when the firm contacted other student organization websites to get more links. Since they had seen authoritative places such as the university already linking to the resource center, it was a much easier ask.

All in all, this was a perfectly executed content/resource link-building technique that can be repeated with the right time, effort, and attention. Now, this example is not easily replicable in the sense that you need a compelling topic, a library of content on that topic, and a good list of organizations that would find that topic interesting. However, it does illuminate a path forward that you can take with your off-page strategy should you so choose.

Keep Diversifying

Local link building, or building links on other businesses' websites that are in your area, can be a great way to diversify your link portfolio while telling Google and consumers a lot about your business. Local link-building campaigns are typically smaller in scale, and because you are reaching out to other businesses in your community, there is an immediate hook that helps to give you a foot in the door.

Another type of project for you to consider is leveraging community opportunities as a way to build links. This can come in many forms. At BluShark, we have done everything for our clients, from running food drives and toy drives around the holidays to bike giveaways for kids and 5K races. You may be thinking, *That sounds crazy; I don't have the time to spend on a project like that.* Of the clients that come to us, 80 percent do not have an existing community development project happening.

We work to find easy opportunities for sponsorships that we can scale to include other businesses in the area. Let's take the food drive example. Starting from scratch, our team put together a list of local businesses within thirty miles of our client's office. These businesses included grocery stores, doctors' offices, bars and restaurants, gyms—you name it. We called, emailed, and texted all of these businesses, explaining that we were putting together a food drive.

Would your business be willing to host a drop box? Our client would provide the box, pick up the food, and post on social media about the business that was participating. All we asked for in return was a page on their blog explaining the food drive with a link back to our site. This has worked time and time again because there is a reason for the business to link to you.

Another reason to consider a project like this is that Google appreciates the local links that you build. It understands your market and its internet ecosystem. The more signals you can send to Google that you are located in a market, even though they are backlinks from other local organizations, the more likely it is to associate you with that market. There are local and organic ranking dividends to running a local community development link-building project. Think outside the box, research local community events that you can cosponsor or get behind, and start putting together a list of businesses you can contact. While it seems daunting, your ability to get a diverse set of links from a single project will pay serious dividends.

Generating links from sources such as .edu and .gov websites can be extremely challenging, so it is up to search marketers to come up with content that these websites like and appreciate so they are willing to link to your site. One link-building strategy that has received significant attention—both praise and criticism—because of its excessive use is scholarship campaigns.

Scholarship campaigns entail offering a college student anywhere from $1,000 to $20,000 to put toward their education. Usually, a scholarship application will entail a transcript and an essay that a student can submit to a business. The business selects a winner and cuts a check. The reason this is such an effective off-page SEO campaign is that it offers something to the university that it can give to its students: money.

Most university websites have an outside scholarships page that you can request your scholarship be added to. All of those lists link back to the website of the company that provides the scholarship. Early on, before everyone was doing a scholarship campaign, I got over one hundred unique links from universities across the country. Of course, you had to build a list, call and email all these schools, and follow up the next year to make sure the link remained up. However, the benefits of running this campaign compared with the costs can't be overstated.

Scholarship campaigns also drive traffic to the website. A student has to visit the website in order to see the prompt for the essay they need to write. They are going to spend time on the site reading the other requirements and figuring out what to do next. All of this traffic, while not monetizable for your business, is traffic that Google is looking at.

This traffic can be healthy if linked up in the right neighborhoods, which can bring serious benefits to the other pages on your site, such as your money pages. SEO practitioners have run scholarship campaigns into the ground, but if you work with an agency that has existing relationships with universities, they can still be fruitful. Many SEO practitioners will say that Google no longer credits scholarship .edu links in the same way, and while that may be true, we do have evidence that they continue to drive traffic and contribute to the overall health of a backlink portfolio. Consider this when thinking about launching your own scholarship campaign.

Focus on What Google Likes

Earlier, we discussed that Google does not like paid links. If a website has a button that says "Pay to list your content," that is not a website you want your content listed on. That being said, SEO practitioners understand that some places on the internet are pay-to-play. Here is where pay-to-play blogs come in. These are blogs in which you or they write the content with a link to your website in exchange for a fee.

The good ones will not publicly advertise these schemes. Instead, you need to contact the blog or editor directly to get pricing on having your content listed on their sites. You may have received emails from SEO practitioners claiming they can get you a link or an article in *The New York Times* or something of that nature. These individuals may have a connection or way of placing your content on these news or blog sites. Be very careful with paying to have blogs listed. Use your judgment along with the tools we have discussed when determining if this is a blog you should be found in.

Find out if the link will be nofollow or dofollow, as that typically impacts price. Learn about the relationship the person publishing your link has with the blog or news site itself. If it seems shady, then it most likely is. Many people have come to me saying they paid a nominal fee to get a blog put up on an authoritative website, only to receive the link and then have it changed to a different website the moment someone else paid the provider. Keep this in mind, as the world of paying for blogs can be ripe with fraud.

Some SEO agencies may have a PBN. PBNs are a set of websites, usually twenty or more, that a single webmaster controls. That webmaster is able to place links on their network of sites as they see fit, free of charge. There is a great deal of risk with PBNs, and you should approach them with great care.

Google is not stupid. It can detect nuances and connections between websites that humans can't. A well-groomed PBN can be extremely powerful, but a poor one can be an absolute disaster if you get it wrong. Having a paid blog strategy is a good way to diversify and acquire higher-authority links that you may not have been able to get otherwise. However, if this is the only strategy you are deploying for your off-page SEO, it will be tough to succeed.

Sponsorships are another way to build links for a fee. There are quite a few sponsorship opportunities out there, from environmental organizations to your kid's little league baseball team. Many of these organizations have websites that can link back to yours. Different from an impact blog, sponsorships are opportunities where you can pay a fee and have your logo or name hyperlinked on the sponsoring organization's website.

What you can do to find these is run a series of Google searches to try to find topical sponsorships. If you are an accident attorney, look to the Brain Injury Association of America or a similar organization. If you are a DUI lawyer, look to Mothers Against Drunk Driving or other local drunk driving organizations. Can you pay to sponsor an event such an organization is hosting in exchange for a link on its website? Evaluate potential sponsorship websites with a fine-tooth comb, as they are not created equally. You don't want to end up paying $10,000 to sponsor a dinner in exchange for a link on a website that has little to no domain authority. From an SEO perspective, make sure to check the linking website data to ensure you are getting what you are paying for.

Tactics to Avoid or Try

One off-page SEO tactic we see a lot is the use of press releases and other content distribution services to build links. There are a ton of different services you can use for press releases, all with different website distribution networks, as well as different rules on the type of link that can be included. I always tell clients when evaluating a press release service to check how long the articles stay up. There are quite a few services out there where, after a month or sometimes even a week, the article is removed from the websites the press release was distributed to.

Further, some distributions will advertise the ability to include a link in the article (or multiple links), but when the articles are pushed out, the links are not hyperlinked. If the link is not hyperlinked, then it is technically not a link. Google will not be able to associate any authority to it, and it is effectively worthless. Press release services are a dime a dozen. Good services will help you get a volume of backlinks in a very timely manner. However, the nature of those links should be heavily scrutinized.

I have seen a lot of law firms waste thousands of dollars on press releases that never moved the needle or no longer exist. For that reason, consider press releases as a way to quickly generate a lot of links from a lot of referring domains, but this should not be your only off-page strategy. Further, if you are using PR services, you must monitor the links that are being built to ensure they are links you actually want, that they stay up, and that the number correlates to what the press release service promised. Ask your SEO agency three months after the fact if the press release links are still up. This will give you insight into how effective the services or platforms they are using actually are.

Another practical link-building strategy is leveraging any other digital or nondigital assets you may have for links. A good example of this is podcast and video link building. If you are running a podcast, there is a high probability that you will have special guests on every episode or from time to time. Either way, those special guests will most likely have a website to which they post content.

If you have a guest on your podcast or you are a guest on another podcast, you should be asking for a link back to your website from theirs. Not only is it good for your brand, but you can also position this request as the best possible scenario for user experience. Asking if someone could include a link on their website in the podcast description is an easy ask, and that link is an easy way for people to learn more about you and your business.

With regard to video, there are quite a few video directories or submission platforms on which you can create profiles. These websites are typically of decent authority, and it is quick and easy to get your videos added and a profile made. Think about other assets you have. Are there other ways you could leverage them to build backlinks? Would mentioning any of these assets result in more successful link placements? Consider questions like this when you are building your off-page SEO strategy.

The Future of Link Building

One thing that SEO specialists are constantly doing is trying to look toward the future and predict, as best they can, what Google is looking for. When it comes to off-page SEO, we know a lot about what Google doesn't want, and a lot of that comes from the complicated history it has had with link building. What is most interesting to us is where the technology of the crawl and algorithm will go in the next five years.

Right now, we know Google relies on the literal code of a web page to pick up on a hyperlink. In theory, it also relies on that code to determine how much authority, if any, to pass from one website to the other. However, what happens if the search crawler gets smart enough to associate a brand or a name with a URL? What happens if you no longer need the actual hyperlink to get "credit" or an endorsement, as a mention of your brand or name accomplishes that same goal?

It is not outside the realm of possibility that the search algorithm and crawlers will get sophisticated enough to accomplish this task. At that point, instead of persuading individuals to post a link to your website, it will be about how and where you can get mentioned on the web. While many of the proven link-building strategies we have discussed would still work in an environment like this, such a development may shift resources in terms of how we think about off-page SEO and link-building projects overall.

Google is already allegedly sophisticated enough to ignore certain links. We know this because the disavow tool has become obsolete and the values Google was prescribing to links as we built them have changed. Understanding the search engine's interactions with your brand outside of your website is critical for SEO success.

You need to have an overall link-building strategy for your website, and when pages are struggling to see results, you need to deploy link building as a way to move those pages higher in the search results. We know that link building is one of the more difficult things to do. After all, who likes cold-calling companies and asking them to link back to your website? At the same time, it is a necessary process for you to grow your business and see success online.

Turning Strategy into Action

Building a successful off-page strategy takes time, creativity, and persistence, but the end results are worth the work. Every tactic, from professional directories to outreach campaigns, has its place in your strategy when used effectively.

Talk to your agency about what off-page SEO tactics it is deploying. Ask how it sees the future of link building or how it stays on top of the links your competition is building. Always ask for links and keep trying to come up with resources you can put on your site that people actually want to link to. Link building is one of the most important but often overlooked components of SEO, so always be building links.

CHAPTER 4

CONTENT IS
STILL KING

A firm owner once asked me why they hadn't seen results from our SEO work. My answer was that it had only been two months, and SEO is a long game. The truth is, many people misunderstand what search engine optimization actually is.

When it comes to search marketing, you can either pay for quick results with ads like LSAs or PPC, or you can invest in organic growth through SEO. Paid ads are like flipping a light switch. As soon as you turn them on, you'll see activity, but only as long as you keep paying. SEO, on the other hand, is like building a house. It takes time, structure, and patience.

The foundation of this house is your website's technical optimization: the coding, structure, and schema markup that make it stable. Strong content forms the walls, giving shape and substance. Link-building serves as the roof, offering protection against competitors. And local search optimization is the furniture and fixtures that transform a shell into a livable home. When all these pieces come together, the house is complete. But it can't be built in two months.

This same principle applies directly to business, especially in industries built on trust and value, like law. Before someone hires you or commits to your brand, you have to prove you can deliver meaningful value consistently. One of the best ways to do this is through content.

Content is more than just words on a page. It's how you demonstrate expertise, build trust, and create connection before a client ever picks up the phone. In this chapter, we'll explore how content became such a powerful driver in SEO, why Google's updates have made quality more important than ever, and how to create the kind of content that not only ranks but also resonates.

It's a Balancing Act

In this chapter, we'll look at the evolution of content in the world of SEO. We'll break down key Google updates and highlight best practices that shape how content should be created and optimized today. You'll learn the differences between various keyword types, how to choose and use them effectively, and how to put on-page SEO tactics into action.

You might be wondering, *Isn't that all there is to it?* Not quite. While selecting strong keywords and writing content that brings value is essential, it's only part of the puzzle. How your content connects with other pages on your site, how your keyword strategy fits into broader variations, and how you organize your site into content silos all play a huge role in driving SEO performance. Simply focusing on keywords and ranking terms isn't enough. You also need a smart structure that supports discoverability and relevance sitewide.

So, what exactly does drafting high-quality content really mean? There's no question that you need it, but how do you go about creating it? The first step in this process is to begin drafting your keyword list. Later, we'll walk through an exercise that helps to identify keywords that you can bid on for paid ads. Here, we will be digging even deeper into those keywords. Instead of focusing on match types, we will concentrate on variations and questions that we believe our customers are searching for. It all comes back to providing benefits to the internet. If your page of content does that, you will be in good shape. If it doesn't and is posted purely for the purposes of driving website traffic, you will be in trouble with Google.

Content is a constant balancing act. You are balancing the need for keywords and clarifying to the algorithm what you want to be found for. You are balancing user experience while ensuring you don't alienate people with excessive content or inappropriate messaging. And you are balancing the necessity to educate and inform to help solve the reader's problem so they are encouraged to take the next step in reaching out to you.

If any aspect of this balance is off, you will face challenges with rankings or conversions. We've already discussed the importance of providing value and benefits to your readers. However, it's equally vital to create an enjoyable experience during a time that is undoubtedly unpleasant for them while establishing your brand as an industry expert. Let's explore the best way to achieve this mission.

How Do I Write Content That Google Likes?

Since its search engine was released, Google has relied on pages of content to pull the best possible result for each search. Content really serves as a benchmark for the search engine to understand what a page is about and what it should be found for. However, Google has had a rocky relationship with content. We have all heard that "content is king." But is it? What does that mean?

How do I write content that Google likes? To understand this, we need to dive into the history of Google and its content. We want to understand its past relationship with content and, to the best of our ability, predict where content is going next.

When I launched my first website, my content was absolutely awful! I will be the first to admit that the phrase *a DC DUI lawyer* was in there exactly like that twenty-five times. I did this because I knew that it was necessary for my page to rank. The more you spammed it with keywords, the more likely it was that Google would pull your web page.

Those days are long gone, and in fact, spammy content practices can cause you to end up in the doghouse with Google. The first major update that Google rolled out to combat content spam was the Panda update. Launched in 2011, this was intended to combat content spam on the internet. Before Panda, there really wasn't a true traffic cop on the content front. People had entire websites of duplicate content. Pages were being created for the sake of search traffic instead of adding value to the internet (doorway pages) and spamming keywords to high heaven, along with many other spammy content practices.

Google had to crack down, and Panda was an early attempt to do so. Google explained Panda in the following way: "This update is designed to reduce rankings for low-quality sites—sites which are low-value add for users, copy content from other websites or sites that are just not very useful. At the same time, it will provide better rankings for high-quality sites—sites with original content and information such as research, in-depth reports, thoughtful analysis and so on."[2] If you had spammy content or were using shady third-party sources to draft your content after this update rolled out, you were in a world of hurt.

What Google Pays Attention To

As Google continued to evolve in how it viewed pages of content, its understanding of searchers' needs also began to evolve. In 2014, Google announced "Your Money or Your Life" (YMYL). The company stated, "Some topics require different standards for quality than others. For example, some topics could significantly impact the health, financial stability, or safety of people, or the welfare or well-being of society. We call such topics "Your Money or Your Life," or YMYL."[3]

Google pays extra special attention to YMYL pages because they directly contribute to the future well-being of the searcher. This is a trend that we typically see with Google. It identifies categories of websites that impact people's lives directly and pays extra attention to those websites. Spam on YMYL websites will be met with an iron fist, and it can be difficult to recover once you are in Google jail. Some common examples of websites that were put under the microscope when Google announced YMYL include those regarding finances, health and safety, fitness and nutrition, and housing.

Legal websites are absolutely in the YMYL category. Since people are making buying decisions that will greatly impact their future, we have to take great care when writing legal marketing content. Google will be looking at this content under a microscope, so the more you

---

2   "Finding More High-Quality Sites in Search," Google, February 24, 2011, https://googleblog.blogspot.com/2011/02/finding-more-high-quality-sites-in.html.

3   "Search Quality Rater Guidelines: An Overview," Google, November 2023, https://services.google.com/fh/files/misc/hsw-sqrg.pdf.

can draft authoritative content that adds value to the internet, the better off you will be.

E-A-T stands for "expertise, authoritativeness, and trustworthiness." When Google announced the E-A-T rollout, it was telling us what it was looking for in our content. In the YMYL rollout, it was telling us which content needs to have serious tender love and care for it to rank and perform well. With E-A-T, it was telling us what we had to show on a page of content for it to rank.

When it rolled out E-A-T, Google commented, "What kind of expertise is required for the page to achieve its purpose well? The standard for expertise depends on the topic of the page."[4] A classic cryptic Google response. What it is saying here is that, depending on the type of website (financial, legal, medical, or otherwise), the standard for expertise has to change. Because there are various levels of expertise in each of these industries, you need to demonstrate you are the expert in yours. So, how do you go about doing that?

How to E-A-T Well

There are different ways to demonstrate your E-A-T to the search engine. One way is through your content. The more authoritative and trustworthy your content is, the more Google will see you as the expert in the field. There are quite a few ways you should be telling Google about your E-A-T.

Having up-to-date legal information on your content pages is critical for demonstrating to Google that you are the authority on what you are writing about. Include statute information on the page, cite legal code, and generally work to educate the user about the topic

---

4   "Google Guidelines Quality Rater 2020," Google, October 2020, https://smart-visibil-ite.fr/wp-content/uploads/2021/05/searchqualityevaluatorguidelines.pdf.

you are writing on. If the page consists of marketing copy telling the reader to call you every other line, that is not going to demonstrate expertise or authority to Google.

Further, having libraries of content on a single topic that all meet the criteria of authoritative content will demonstrate to Google that you are the authority in your field. If you have twenty-five pages on the DUI case process, what happens after an arrest, different penalties for different levels of offenses, etc., Google will see you as more of an authority on DUI than someone with a single DUI lawyer page. When Google announced E-A-T, it specifically mentioned legal websites. It stated, "High E-A-T financial advice, legal advice, tax advice etc. should come from trustworthy sources and be maintained and updated regularly."

Some firms are using AI tools to help draft their legal content, but this comes with risks if you aren't smart about it. Google allows AI-generated content as long as it is helpful, accurate, and reader-focused. In YMYL fields like law, though, those standards are even higher. Any AI-assisted content must be carefully reviewed for legal accuracy, tone, and relevance. While AI can assist your content creation, it shouldn't replace the knowledge and experience that only a legal professional can provide. Use AI as a tool to support your content efforts, not a shortcut.

Once Google has identified your legal website in the high E-A-T category, you need to do everything possible to show them you are the expert. One thing we have done that has worked well is to implement more structured data that includes credentials, awards, and accolades, even in some cases where people went to school. This is especially true in the medical frontier—the amount of structured data you can add to signal to Google that you are the expert and authority on the subject matter you are writing about is critical for success.

Make sure you have a built-out "About Me" page that lists all your awards and accolades. Consider adding authorship to your website so that Google knows who is writing the content. All of these things send signals to Google that you are the expert, have the authority, and deserve to be trusted with the traffic they send your way.

When E-A-T was first launched and coupled with YMYL, certain websites got absolutely slaughtered. Local blogs written by amateurs, which were giving health advice, such as what to do with your dysfunctional thirteen-year-old, or telling you which stocks to invest in, took serious hits. This makes complete sense. Again, Google wants to protect the user's money and life as much as it possibly can.

Later, Google announced E-E-A-T, also known as "Double E-A-T," which added an extra E that stands for "experience." Google states: "Now to better assess our results, E-A-T is gaining an E: experience. Does content also demonstrate that it was produced with some degree of experience, such as with actual use of a product, having actually visited a place or communicating what a person experienced? There are some situations where really what you value most is content produced by someone who has first-hand, life experience on the topic at hand."[5] With this announcement, it further emphasized the need to highlight current and past experiences on your website. Case results and longer bios that include a history of your experience all help to deliver the information Google is looking for.

---

5   "Our Latest Update to the Quality Rater Guidelines: E-A-T Gets an Extra E for Experience," Google, December 2022, https://developers.google.com/search/blog/2022/12/google-raters-guidelines-e-e-a-t.

The Release of BERT

Bidirectional encoder representations from transformers (BERT) was released in October 2019. This term may seem like a mouthful—because it is—but behind the technical mumbo jumbo, the release of BERT was a pivotal moment in Google's lifetime. BERT was intended to better understand the intent of a searcher's query.

BERT leverages neural network–based techniques for better and more natural language process pre-training. BERT, at its core, is a natural language processing (NLP) model that, when overlayed with all the data Google has, makes for an extremely powerful AI. Google made BERT open source, so anyone can train it as an NLP model. BERT is learning every day from the billions of searches people are entering on Google.

It is processing all of those queries and making its model better based on those results. BERT has the ability to train its language model based on entire sets of words in a sentence or a search, which means it undergoes bidirectional training. Historically, Google had relied on the order of words to understand the meaning of a search.

Google gives us this example to see BERT in action: "For example, the word 'bank' would have the same context-free representation in 'bank account' and 'bank of the river.' Contextual models instead generate a representation of each word that is based on the other words in the sentence. For example, in the sentence 'I accessed the bank account,' a unidirectional contextual model would represent 'bank' based on 'I accessed the' but not 'account.' However, BERT represents 'bank' using both its previous and next context — '*I accessed the … account.*'"[6] This may sound confusing, but all it means is Google

---

6   "Open Sourcing BERT: State-of-the-Art Pre-Training for Natural Language Processing," Google, November 2018, https://research.google/blog/open-sourcing-bert-state-of-the-art-pre-training-for-natural-language-processing/.

is evolving how it interprets the words in a search. It is only a matter of time before it can better process and understand the content you write for your website.

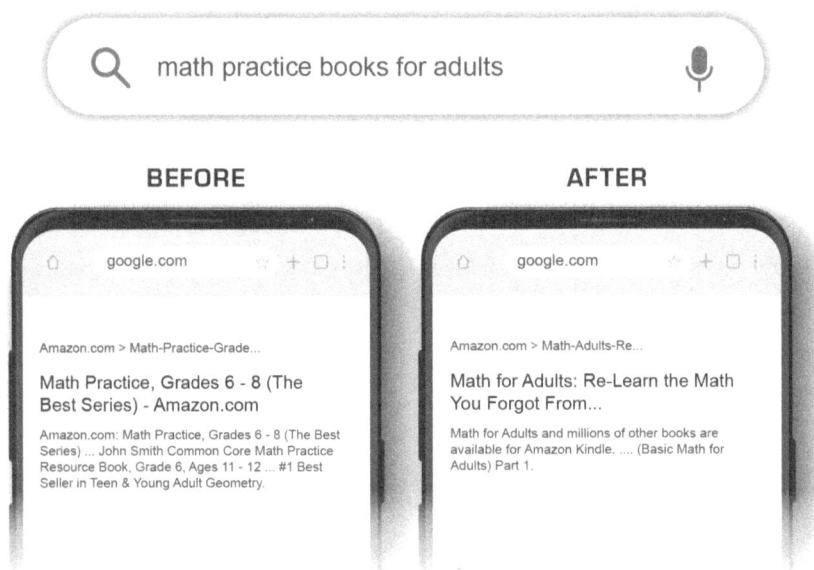

Many people tell me, "This is cool, but what does it mean for my website and my business?" As mentioned many times previously, people are searching for what they think they need to search in order for the result they want to appear. What BERT does is pick up on more contextual triggers in the search itself, thereby delivering a more accurate interpretation of the search terms.

As BERT continues to evolve, it will have better accuracy. Eventually, users will move to search for what is most natural to them instead of what they think they need to search for to generate a result. For example, it is entirely possible within the next five years that someone looking for an Atlanta car accident lawyer does not need to search those words exactly to find the lawyer they need.

If this model continues to evolve, it could result in this user searching for "I was in a car accident" as they are sitting in their apartment in Atlanta. Google will understand what the user is looking for and needs from that search. The search is much more natural than "Atlanta car accident lawyer," and how people are searching could begin to change.

Writing Content That Ranks

Creating content that resonates with both readers and Google—whether it's written by a human, generated with the help of AI, or a combination of the two—requires a balance of relevance, authority, and structure. Google's algorithms have evolved, so our approach to content must evolve as well. Prioritizing information that builds trust and establishes authority is essential to pleasing Google, but it's especially important for legal websites. Gone are the days of keyword stuffing and generic copy—now, your content must be intentional.

This brings us to a very important topic—keywords.

CHAPTER 5

THE KEY TO KEYWORDS

Keywords are the connecting hub between what people are searching for and your website. Every search starts with the keywords a searcher enters. Currently, that means they enter what they think they need to search in order to generate the search result that they want. There are three main types of keywords: branded keywords, money keywords, and long-tail keywords.

The most basic of these to understand are branded keywords. Branded keywords are keywords that literally contain your brand name. Think of someone searching for Air Jordan shoes. That person is very specifically looking for the Air Jordan brand. Another example could be "your firm name + reviews." That is a branded search by someone who most likely is checking out the reputation of your firm.

Money keywords are instances where the searcher's intent is to make a purchase or buying decision. This could be a term like "Car accident lawyer near me." In this instance, the searcher is most likely looking to take the next step with a car accident lawyer. That "near me" indicates they may be willing to travel to learn about the next steps.

Another example could be "DUI lawyer for my case." Very clearly, the searcher has a DUI (a key qualifier for a DUI case), is interested in a lawyer, and is looking to make a buying decision soon. Money keywords are typically more competitive. Since they are buying keywords, all firms are competing for these keywords, and they will be the most expensive in a paid ads campaign.

Long-tail keywords are informational searches. Usually, people who are doing long-tail searches are closer to the top of the funnel. They may be looking for information about their case before deciding to call. Two examples of a long-tail search are "How long will my car accident case take?" or "Steps for handling your own car accident case." In both of these examples, the searcher is looking for more information about a topic—in this case, their car accident.

Depending on the situation, they may eventually decide they need a car accident lawyer and search for it. They just searched a money keyword, and you can see how a searcher's buyer journey develops. Another example in the family law space could be "Steps to take before filing for a divorce" or "Best-case scenario for my child custody case." In both of these examples, the searcher is trying to locate information that is valuable to them. This is why, with every page of content you write, you should keep in mind that it should add value to the internet. Writing pages for the sake of writing pages does not work and eventually will cost you a lot of time and money.

Long-tail keywords will continue to be a topic of discussion. As generative AI gets more advanced, it is very possible that long-tail keyword traffic will drop off. However, as of right now, it is important to have pages that touch on long-tail keywords. These pages will drive valuable traffic and could eventually lead to a conversion.

Keyword strategy goes deeper than these components, though. You must also include variations to capture a wider range of search intent and think about how all keyword types inform your content strategy.

Keyword Variations

While thinking about your keywords, it is also important to consider other variations of those keywords that people may be searching. Keyword variations are word choice selections that could alter a search result but carry the same meaning. Historically, you would need to put these variations throughout the page to be found for them. However, as we just discussed, the algorithm is getting better at understanding the meaning of words and sentences. Still, it is important to develop possible variations to keywords so that you can add them throughout your content. This also helps to break up using the same key term over and over again, making the page sound more natural.

Let's take an example keyword and do a simple exercise to help you figure out your keyword variations. Start by writing out your keyword. In this example, we'll use "Atlanta divorce lawyer." Now, under each word, list out all the possible variations for that word:

- Atlanta: Atl, Atlanta, GA, In Atlanta

- Divorce: Dissolution of marriage, Split with wife/husband, End marriage, Legal breakup, etc.

- Lawyer: Attorney, Law firm, Attorneys, Lawyers

If you do this with each of your keywords, you'll quickly build a robust list of potential keyword variations. Even better, you'll start to notice patterns and trends across your terms—insights that will help you develop a stronger, more strategic approach to optimization.

Developing Keyword Lists

Before starting to write pages of content, you first need to identify the words that you want to be found for. There are countless ways to create this keyword list, but start with what you know. Remember our three different types of keywords. Start with money terms, then work through branded terms, and finally finish with the long-tail search terms you think people are searching.

Take this initial list of keywords and put it through the Keyword Planner in Google to ensure there is enough search volume for the keywords that you have chosen. Do this for each and every practice area keyword you want to target. Performing due diligence during this phase of the process will save you hours and dollars later on. I have come across many SEO strategies that do not work because the keywords that were chosen and the location being targeted are not large enough. There is so little search volume that, even if the website does rank number one, it is extremely difficult to get a return on investment (ROI). If you are concerned about this, consider looking at the populations of the locations you are targeting to ensure a large enough group of people.

Using tools is critical when you are developing your keyword list. You can use the Keyword Planner to start to find additional keyword opportunities and see how competitive the potential keywords you have chosen are. We love using AnswerThePublic, Google Trends, and the "People also ask" section of Google for locating additional content keyword topics. SpyFu, Semrush, and Ahrefs all provide great competitor keyword research tools to learn what keywords your competitors are ranking for. Some of these tools may also provide you with helpful stats on keyword competition level or lead you down a path you otherwise may not have gone down.

How Long Should My Content Be?

When potential clients ask me how long pages of content should be, it can be tricky to answer. On the surface, your content should be as long as it needs to be to accomplish the goal of answering the consumer's questions, conveying experience, expertise, authority, and trustworthiness to Google, and telling the consumer what type of brand you are. Generally speaking, your content should be at least 500 to 750 words. This number is roughly based on historical experiences and what we think Google wants to see.

This is a sliding scale that should adjust according to the page's performance. If a page is not performing well, perhaps adding another 250 words can boost that page in Google's eyes. If all your competition in the market has pages that are 1,500 words and are substantive, perhaps you need to inch closer to that number in order to stay competitive in the market. Let's keep in mind that we do not want to turn users off by having them land on a page that is a giant wall of text.

Since there are so many factors that can influence how long your content should be, the bottom line is you should never just write a page, post it, and let it sit there. That page's performance should be tracked (rankings and traffic, user experience, etc.), so you know how well that page is doing. You should be tracking your competitors to see what they are doing with their content, regarding not just word count but also keyword choices, messaging of their brand, and other things as well. Keep this in mind when you are trying to determine how long your pages of content should be.

Localizing Your Content

Over the years, I have tested many different content strategies. Local SEO is a beast in and of itself. I have learned that there are certain tactics you can deploy on your content for better organic and local SEO performance.

One of these tactics is localizing your content pages. Geomodified searches are searches that include the geographic area. Think "Atlanta criminal lawyer" or "Los Angeles PI lawyer." Those searches include the geographic term (geo) plus the keyword. Some people may only search for the keyword when they are located in a geographic area. Our localized content optimization practices help rank content pages in both of these instances. So, what do we mean by localizing content?

It isn't just about including the name of the geographic area that you want to rank in a bunch of times (while it should be in there a few times). Really, it comes down to ensuring you have a page that talks about your practice areas in the context of those cities:

- What does it mean to get in a car accident on Rodeo Drive?

- Are there local statutes that you should be discussing?

- Are there any local highways or intersections that see a lot of accidents or DUI checkpoints?

- What should someone who is preparing for divorce court know about the location of their hearing?

Include this information as much as you can on the pages of content you write. The more you can localize the content, the more it seems like you know the area and are a local attorney. This increases the probability of conversion greatly and will help to increase rankings. By talking about these different factors, you are showing Google you have local experience and are a trusted source for local legal information.

There is no need for overkill here. You do not need to write a page of content on every zip code in a city. (I have seen some firms do this, and it is a complete disaster.) The best way to test if you need to write a specific localized page of content for a geographic area is by running a Google search. Google "your geo + keyword" and see what comes up. Are the results that are listed home pages? Are these pages specific to the location you are thinking of writing about? (An easy way to check this is by looking at the URL—does it list the geo name?)

If the answer to these questions is yes, you need to write a unique page of content for that "geo + practice area" in order to be competitive in the market. If you do start to create overlapping content pages that are saying the same thing, Google will get confused. It will not know which page to show, and it will cause fluctuations and drops in rankings. Making sure you are seizing on any available opportunity while not spamming the internet unnecessarily with content that doesn't add value to the internet is a balancing act you will need to continually do.

Keywords That Connect

Content planning starts with keyword planning. The more robust your keyword list, the more of a road map you have for developing content that encompasses both long-tail and money keywords. Make sure your content is long enough to show your expertise and authority, and bring in local elements to show Google and your audience that you are trustworthy in the area you are seeking to represent.

Keywords are the foundation of an effective content strategy, and they require variation and local relevance to reach their intended audience. A smart keyword strategy married with quality content is key to keeping Google happy and ensuring your content is seen by searchers.

CHAPTER 6

OPTIMIZE YOUR WEBSITE CONTENT

I saw a post recently from my friend Jonathan Pollard, founder of Pollard PLLC, saying that résumé gaps aren't relevant. I like Jonathan a lot, but I disagree totally. Between Price Benowitz LLP and BluShark Digital, I currently manage three hundred employees and have hired hundreds more throughout my career. Through these experiences, I've learned firsthand that a résumé gap isn't necessarily a reason not to hire someone, but it does deserve an explanation.

If your gap occurred because you spent time caring for a family member or raising your young kids, that's incredibly valuable to me. It signals that you prioritize family and are willing to make sacrifices for important things in life. That kind of gap makes me even more inclined to hire you.

However, not all résumé gaps are equally reassuring. Sometimes, they can mask issues that would influence a hiring decision:

- Did you leave your last job on good terms, or did you burn bridges?

- Are you financially independent, making work optional, which might affect your motivation?

A résumé gap isn't necessarily a red flag, but it's definitely a flag, and understanding what color it is can make all the difference. Am I being unreasonable for wanting clarity?

Just as a résumé gap needs context, clarity, and honest storytelling to convey the right message, your website content needs precisely the same treatment. Visitors to your website, such as potential employers reviewing résumés, are actively looking for reasons to engage or disengage. Vague or unclear content acts like unexplained gaps, raising unnecessary flags and questions that might deter visitors from converting into customers or clients.

Optimizing your website content means clearly communicating your value, purpose, and credibility without leaving visitors wondering or filling in gaps with their assumptions. This chapter will guide you through the strategies for crafting precise, transparent, and engaging content—content that tells your audience exactly who you are, why you matter, and why they should trust you.

The Basics of On-Page SEO

On-page SEO is the practice of optimizing a website's content for the purpose of improving its ranking. We will be briefly discussing the most important on-page SEO factors, what you need to know about them, and a checklist you can use to make sure all on-page SEO factors are met during the page publishing process. A key aspect of on-page SEO is establishing a scalable process for publishing pages. Like a pilot armed with their pre-takeoff checklist, you will be ready for SEO takeoff.

One big component of on-page SEO is keyword usage. We have already discussed keywords and keyword types in great detail, but a critical component of on-page SEO is how you use those keywords. You want to sprinkle in the exact keywords a few times throughout the page. You want this to sound as natural as possible, so think about your word choice as you put these keywords in.

You will also want to consider your keyword variations or long-tail phrase keywords that you want to include. Again, Google is getting much smarter at how it is reading and interpreting the words on a page. Because of this, the contextual triggers it understands are at a level never seen before. It is not necessary to include exact long-tail queries. If the words are in the sentence, Google should be able to pick up and understand the meaning of those words. Of course, if you have an opportunity to include a great long-tail phrase, do it, but this should never prevent you from creating natural-sounding content.

Another big component of on-page SEO is page structure. Utilizing headings and the right heading tags as you go down a page is important for SEO success. Headings are in the code as H tags: H1 or heading 1, H2 or heading 2, H3 or heading 3, and so on. There is more weight put on the words in H1s versus H2s and more on H2s versus H3s. You can have multiple H2s or H3s if necessary throughout a page, but you should always only have a single H1.

You need to think about headings as valuable real estate to convey to Google what you want to be found for. That being said, headings should be natural so a user (or Google) is not turned off by spammy headings. Headings should flow down the page like they do in any other book or article. They should make logical sense, and your H2 and H3 headings should include some of those long-tail phrases or keyword variations. Making sure you are thinking about your headings and intentionally using keywords are best practices for on-page SEO.

Another core component of on-page SEO is your title tag. Your title tag is not within the content itself. However, it plays a major role in rankings and click-through rates from the SERP. Every page on your website should have a unique title tag that explains what the page is about. This is not to be confused with the H1 or first heading. The title instead is what appears when you hover over the browser window on your preferred browser. It is also the words that appear in the SERP organic listing:

https://blog.spotibo.com › meta-description-length Traf/mo (us): 1300/1400 - Kw (us): 52/116

6. The meta description length in 2021 - Spotibo SEO ✔

Jan 23, 2021 — The **meta description length** is **between 120 – 158 characters**, up to 920 pixels. See the details below or see a title length limits. Meta ...
★★★★★ Rating: 4.4 · 240 votes

| How long should meta descriptions be? | ⌄ |
| How many characters use in a meta description? | ⌄ |

MOZ DA: 32/100 (+0%) Ref Dom: 387 Ref Links: 1.05K Spam Score: 1%

L: 246 • LD: 1.25K • I: error • Rank: 72.2K • whois </> source • Rank: 1.01M • Adv Disp Ads: 5 • Pub Disp Ads: 0

https://www.brightedge.com › blog › google-increases-... Traf/mo (us): 210/41.90K - Kw (us): 17/5217

7. Google Decreases Meta Description Length | BrightEdge ✔

Previously, the standard maximum **meta description length** was **165 characters**; now **Google** is showing an average of **320 characters** for some of the results on the ...
MOZ DA: 60/100 (+3%) Ref Dom: 7.21K Ref Links: 70.11K Spam Score: 7%

L: 1 • LD: 68.5K • I: error • Rank: 5.65K • whois </> source • Rank: 69.8K • Adv Disp Ads: 62 • Pub Disp Ads: 0

https://seopressor.com › blog › google-title-meta-descri... Traf/mo (us): 190/9300 - Kw (us): 42/1354

8. Google's Title and Meta Descriptions Length (Updated 2020) ✔

Mar 16, 2019 — **Currently**, the title displayed on mobile has **72 characters**, and **meta descriptions** have **172 characters**, which are longer than previously.
MOZ DA: 49/100 (-2%) Ref Dom: 7.59K Ref Links: 380.6K Spam Score: 1%

L: 1.03K • LD: 136K • I: error • Rank: 20.1K • whois </> source • Rank: 204K • Adv Disp Ads: 0 • Pub Disp Ads: 0

Your title tag should include the main keyword that you want that page to be found for. In other words, your car accident title tag may be "geo + car accident lawyer." Your truck accident page may be for a truck accident lawyer in your geo. Additionally, you should know that the first part of your title tag is weighted more than the latter portion of your title tag.

Word choice is critical for maximizing the optimizations you can get from a title tag. Do not be afraid to potentially include keyword variations in the latter part of your title tag. Make sure you know the current title tag character count. This count has changed multiple times throughout the years, and if you go over the character count, Google may not show your preferred title tag.

I have seen countless examples on the search engine where the title tag is cut off or pulling from random headings on the page. This will occur if your title tag is too long or if you do not set a title tag (Google will pick one for you). Your title tag is also an important conversion mechanism. If your title tag looks wonky on the search engine, there is a high probability that the searcher will choose another organic listing over yours. Keep all of these factors in mind as you create your title tags.

Another important on-page SEO and conversion piece is meta descriptions. Like title tags, meta descriptions do not necessarily appear within the content itself. A meta description is a page description you set when the page is published. This description gives a brief overview of what the page is and shows up under the organic listing in the SERP. Your meta description is your biggest conversion opportunity from the SERP. If you have a strong meta description, there is a much higher chance that a searcher will click on your listing over a competitor's.

Your meta description is another opportunity for you to use keywords and keyword variations to signal to Google what you want to be found for. You should always include keywords in your meta; this is a big on-page ranking factor. You only have 160 characters here to make a compelling case as to why someone should click on your organic listing.

Since meta descriptions are an extreme abstract of what the page is about, they rely on keywords you put in your meta description, again prescribing more weight to those than what may be on your content page. Google does reserve the right to pull meta descriptions that it sees as more relevant to a search. However, if you set your meta descriptions properly, it can pay huge dividends down the line. Both meta descriptions and title tags can be set using third-party SEO tools, such as Yoast. Screaming Frog is another tool that scans every page on the site, pulling headings, title tags, meta descriptions, word counts, and other useful pieces of on-page SEO information.

The final on-page SEO technique we will be discussing is internal links. Internal links serve as gateways on your website to other relevant pages. The best example of internal linking is Wikipedia. How many times have you been on Wikipedia only to have come out of your Wiki slumber some five hours later completely educated on the history of anise liquor in eighteenth-century France? The ability for a user to get sucked further into the websites is one of the powers of internal links.

Internal links also show the search engine crawler where to go next. They help guide the crawler to the pages you want them to index, creating an easy crawl environment that the search engines appreciate. Internal links also send authority signals to the internal page you are linking to. In other words, the more times you link internally to a specific page, the more you are telling the search engine that this is an important page.

The anchor text, or the literal words that are hyperlinked on the page, is also a key indicator to Google and its users about the page they are about to land on. You should use money and keyword variations throughout your website on internal links in order to maximize the signals you are sending to the search engine. We want our internal pages to be jumping up and down, screaming, "Find me, find me!" The more you can highlight these pages through internal links, the louder those screams will become.

Now that you have your on-page SEO checklist, it is time to put it to the test. Run a Screaming Frog report on your website and audit all of your meta descriptions, title tags, headings, and internal links. Leveraging these tactics will allow you to find new optimization opportunities that may bring you to the top.

Create Content Silos

Internal links are a fantastic way to guide the search engine crawler and users to deeper pages on your website. We know that Google likes websites that have volumes of content on the subject matter in which they claim to be an expert. However, there are other techniques you can and should use to organize your content on the website in a way that is friendly to users and bots. One of these tactics is to create content silos on your website.

Content silos are a way of managing the volume of content that you may have for a particular practice area. It is not enough to write one page of content on a particular practice area. You need to have a library of content for every practice and subpractice area that you may have. For example, if you are writing about criminal law, you want to have pages on all the different practice areas within criminal law, drug, assault, guns, fraud, etc.

From there, we need to develop libraries of content on each sub-practice area. For example, DUI cases can include

- first offense DUI,

- felony DUI,

- DUI with a CDL,

- DUI with a security clearance,

- field sobriety testing,

- breathalyzer testing, and

- defense strategies in a DUI case.

The list goes on and on. Let's take another example with drugs: possession lawyer, possession with intent, federal drug, meth, cocaine, manufacturing, money laundering in a drug case, etc. All of these topics could have their own 750-word pages that educate the reader about what they are facing.

Content silos start with structuring your URLs and organizing your published pages in the most logical way. Let's take the previous example with the imaginary firm, nicelawyer.com. We need to organize our criminal practice area pages. Our home page, or most authoritative page, should use our main keyword, "criminal lawyer."

Coming off our home page, we have our criminal lawyer practice areas of DUI, assault, drugs, and guns. Since the home page is the parent page to these pages, the URL will look like this: nicelawyer.com/dui-attorney/, nicelawyer.com/drug-attorney/, nicelawyer.com/assault-attorney/, nicelawyer.com/gun-attorney/. All of these pages will be linked on the home page, most likely through a top or side navigation menu.

A parent page should always link to a child page, and a child page should link back up to its parent. Continuing with this example, we have our libraries of content for both DUI and drugs. These subpages should categorically match up to their parent, and their URL will reflect that relationship.

For DUI, the URLs would look something like nicelawyer.com/dui-attorney/first-offense/, nicelawyer.com/dui-attorney/felony/, nicelawyer.com/dui-attorney/CDL/, and so on. For drugs, the URL would look something like this: nicelawyer.com/drug-attorney/PWID/ nicelawyer.com/drug-attorney/possession/, nicelawyer.com/drug-attorney/cocaine/. You are nestling the child page underneath the applicable parent page. By doing so, you are creating a website structure that focuses the user and search bot on one subject and one subject only.

One of the reasons we want to develop content silos is that they funnel users to the most relevant part of the website that is important for their search. Most searchers are not searching for "criminal lawyer," going to the website, and clicking on the DUI tab. Instead, they are searching for a DUI lawyer, and when they land on your site, it is on the DUI-specific page. If, on that page, the menus, the internal links, and all the information are related to DUI, you just provided a positive user experience. The user can navigate to the other important DUI pages you have on that section of the site. They will not be distracted by links to how to prep for an assault case. They have a DUI, and all the information that is presented to them within that silo is relevant to DUIs. By structuring your content in silos, you are creating a positive user experience and giving the search engine an even greater reason to consider you as an expert or authority on a specific subject matter.

Biggest Content No-Nos

SPINNING CONTENT

There are no shortcuts when it comes to creating content. Content is expensive to produce and takes time to do well. Taking shortcuts on your content can lead to disastrous consequences, so let's walk through some of the biggest content no-nos to keep you on track.

Fifteen years ago, I was sitting in my office, and I got an email from someone claiming they could write a hundred pages of content for a hundred dollars. Intrigued, I reached out, and he started to explain his process to me. He would run a search, find competitor websites, put it in a program that rearranged the words, and send back the page.

No, I am not talking about ChatGPT or other generative AI. Instead, this practice of spinning content that is already published on the web has been around for a long time. It is not something you should ever do. You should always ask a content provider how they are producing your content and ensure that it is original copy. Be wary of any schemes to get content quickly, as we know content takes time to produce.

DUPLICATIVE CONTENT

Another common pitfall in the content landscape is duplicative content. Many websites would plagiarize content from other websites or even from themselves and reuse parts or entire pages. No wonder Google does not like duplicative content. Duplicate content adds no value to the internet. The only purpose for that content existing is to drive traffic and manipulate the search engines. For this reason, it is a big no-no. It is worth reiterating again that you should not plagiarize yourself. If you are writing hundreds of locations and practice area pages, that can become difficult, but take great care not to plagiarize. This can lead to serious SEO setbacks and will ultimately harm your business.

AI-GENERATED CONTENT

Now, the topic of conversation is about AI and content. How much AI content is it OK to have before Google gets upset? Since we are in the early days of generative AI, time will tell how much Google cares about AI-generated content. That being said, everything we have talked about in this chapter revolves around the importance of expertise, experience, authority, and trustworthiness, especially as it pertains to content that is related to a searcher's money or well-being.

If you are using generative AI for your content pages, how can Google know your unique experience or why someone should trust you over another website? That human element that goes into a content page is still necessary. Time will tell how much this will evolve, but for the time being, it is important to operate within the confines that Google is signaling to us.

One final story on this. I was at a conference, and someone came up to me, explaining that they had an AI content manual action penalty and Google had sent them a message saying their website had been caught for spam because of AI content. This is an unconfirmed account. However, it does stand to reason that Google is paying attention to this. It will have a way of knowing what is AI-generated and what is not. Furthermore, it will be up to each website owner to assess the risks and rewards associated with AI content. Is it inside the realm of possibility that Google launches another update that starts with a *P,* is named after an animal, and targets AI content? Absolutely. As the discussion continues to shift toward generative AI, it is even more crucial to stay abreast of content trends.

Staying Ahead of the Content Curve

You should now have an overall understanding of the content process, where to start, how to optimize content on a page, and how to structure that content as you publish it to your website. Content is one area that stays the same while changing a great deal at the same time. Having a basic understanding of the different components that comprise content will allow you to stay ahead of the curve and draw your own conclusions on the direction that Google will move in next.

The world of content is constantly evolving, and content is critical for your on-page SEO success. Further, how you set up your website with menus and internal links plays a direct role in how users will interact with your website and how long they will stay there. For these reasons, it is critical that you prioritize your content and website structure and avoid content no-nos to position yourself in the best light possible.

Technical SEO

You can have a website that has hundreds of pages of content and blogs on it and has extremely powerful off-page signals pointing into it, but without a strong technical foundation, that website will have a hard time ranking for competitive search terms. Having a strong technical foundation is critical for overall organic SEO success. In the next chapter, we will discuss the overarching themes of technical SEO.

We will cover important technical SEO topics that you should always consider asking your agency about. We will also go through the best way to move a website from one platform to another. Finally, we will discuss the nuances of technical SEO and why it is so important to have it buttoned up for a successful website. What we will not be doing is discussing how to build and launch a website. At this point,

I think we all understand the importance of having subject matter experts, developers in this instance, work on something as important as your website. That being said, you will have the ammo you need to discuss technical SEO with your developers and ensure it is deployed properly on your website.

Technical SEO touches all other aspects of our work. From paid to local or the obvious organic rankings, technical SEO is a bedrock subject that can't be overlooked. If the technical components of your website are wrong or causing things to function incorrectly, you will lose business. If your website takes too long to load or is not friendly on all devices and browsers, you will lose business. If you have malware or spam on the website, Google will know, and it will be extremely difficult to rank (not to mention the viruses your potential clients may contract). Let's think about technical SEO with a fresh outlook and develop our technical SEO checklists to maximize your results.

CHAPTER 7

IF IT'S NOT INDEXED, IT DOESN'T EXIST

Not long ago, we got hit with one of those emails you never really want to see on a Friday. It was from our integrator at BluShark, and she was turning in her two weeks' notice. My first reaction was, and I quote, "We're screwed."

During the chaos of COVID-19, she'd been a linchpin. She was smart, capable, and everywhere all at once. She wore a ton of hats, but about 60 percent of her job centered on finance. And she was *really* good at it. But here's the kicker: When she left, we realized that almost everything she knew—every workflow, every trick, every nuance—was locked up in her head. No documentation. No systems. No backup plan.

So when she walked out the door, all that knowledge walked with her. We didn't have the luxury of time, so we acted fast. I called up a friend in financial recruiting, spent the weekend interviewing candidates, and by Monday morning, we had a new head of finance ready to roll.

That experience taught me (again) a few really valuable lessons:

- You need to be able to move quickly when gaps open up.

- A single point of failure is a business risk you can't afford.

- Systems and documentation aren't luxuries. They're survival tools.

- If you have someone doing it all without building a team or a knowledge base, you're basically gambling with your company's future.

Now, why open a chapter on website indexing with this story? Because your website works the same way. If Google is the recruiter trying to figure out what your site knows, and everything it needs to know is poorly linked, buried in random corners, or not documented in a structured way, then your site is the equivalent of that amazing but undocumented employee. All the value is there, but no one can access it.

Indexing isn't just about getting your pages in Google. It's about making sure the knowledge on your site is discoverable, understandable, and connected. So, let's dig into how to do that. Because a website without proper indexing? That's a business running blind.

What It Takes to Rank

A web page must be indexed for it to rank.

What do we mean by that? We don't mean that a paper copy of the web page needs to be printed and filed with your local library.

Instead, we mean that the search engine has an inventory of every page of content, every image, and every video on your website. The search engine can't rank number one what it does not have indexed. The user can't find the web page from the search engine if it is not indexed. So, it is first critical to understand the fundamentals of indexing, how search engines index pages, and why it is important in the grand scheme of technical SEO.

You may be wondering, *Well, how does Google go about indexing pages, and what happens if it is unable to index a page on my site?* There are a few different ways in which a page can be indexed by Google. The first and most common is that the web page is crawled by the search engine. Google is constantly crawling and archiving every website on the internet (that it can access or chooses to access). That crawl bot will go through every page on your site, following the links, images, and the like to create information it can store in its database.

From there, when a search query is conducted, millions of signals are triggered, and the algorithm determines which page to show on the SERP. If, during the crawl, the bot encounters problems and is unable to reach a page, or if a link leads to a "page not found" error, the crawl may stop or may not be fully completed. As SEO practitioners, it is our job to ensure the bot has access to all the pages we want it to have access to. Strategically, there may be a time when you choose not to index a page, maybe a pay-per-click (PPC) landing page. However, you need to understand and master the crawled content that Google is associating with your website.

Another common way Google indexes content is through a site map. Think of site maps as an opportunity for you to tell Google what is on your site and how it is organized. Site maps are created in the background of your website and are almost like a table of contents for the search engine to follow and understand. Your developer should be able to enable site map creation so that when a new page of content is added to your website, it is automatically added to the site map. You can then take this site map and manually submit it to Google Search Console.

This will ensure that the URLs, so long as there are no issues with your site map, will be indexed on Google. In Search Console, you can also submit an individual URL for indexing if there is a particular page that is struggling to be indexed. Google typically trusts site maps but does verify them. Discrepancies with your site map can cause major indexing issues, so it is important to keep these up to date and accurate. If your site map is telling Google URLs that it is unable to find itself in its own crawl, you almost certainly will have trouble.

Depending on the size and scope of your website, it may make sense to submit multiple site maps to Google. Many people will create separate site maps for their blog pages versus their regular content pages as a way of ensuring every page is indexed. Many will also submit an image site map to get their images indexed in Google Images. Finally, if you are running a multi-language property, it may make sense for you to submit a separate site map for the different languages you have content for. The goal here is to organize your content in a way that Google can crawl and understand.

Three Nonnegotiables

In 2023, Google announced that it would be switching to a mobile-first index. What this means is that a page must be indexed on mobile for it to show up in the search results at all. In other words, if you created a desktop-only version of a web page, there is a high probability that the page will not be indexed. If you have a separate mobile website (m.xyz.com), you need to pay particular attention to this. If there are discrepancies between the indexed URLs on your mobile site and your desktop site, Google will get confused about which pages to index; multiples can be indexed, and chaos ensues.

I was once at a conference when someone came up to me and asked why his website wasn't ranking. I told him there were probably a number of reasons his website wasn't ranking, but to first check and see if all his web pages were indexed. He had no idea what that meant, so I showed him a quick trick: Enter "site:websiteurl.com" into Google, using his site's URL. He took the time at the booth to do it, and sure enough, there were zero results.

He asked me how this could be possible. He had a three-hundred-page website he was paying $2,000 a month for. After a five-minute investigation, we saw in the source code that the entire website was set to noindex, nofollow. Google was being told not to crawl the website. I tell you this story to remind everyone that sometimes the largest technical SEO issues are hidden in plain sight.

Other common crawl and indexing issues that we come across include errors such as 404s, or "page not found" errors, in your site map. You don't want to tell Google that you have pages on your website that do not work. Additionally, having duplicate page URLs, failing to remove pages from your site map that have been removed from the site, or having basic typos in your live site URL versus your site map can cause significant SEO indexing issues. Run the site: Check on your website to make sure everything is indexing as it should.

Robots.txt files can be powerful tools for directly telling a search engine crawl what you want it to crawl and what you do not want it to crawl. There may be, for example, a page that aggregates all of your blogs into a single page. This URL would not need to be indexed; however, you want to make sure all of your blogs are indexed. In this example, you could use the robots file to direct the search crawler where you want it to go.

It should be noted that if these files are not done properly, then the consequences are disastrous. Unless you are having issues with indexing, your robots file is most likely in good shape. If you are having indexing issues, check with your webmaster and request that they pull the file. Understand what is being excluded from search engine crawls and why.

Google Search Console, formerly Google Webmaster Tools, is a critical set of tools that you need to understand to be successful at technical SEO. As mentioned previously, Search Console is the place to submit an individual URL for indexing, check if there are any indexing errors on the website, submit your site map(s), and receive communications from Google about your website. If Search Console is set up properly, the information it provides serves as a check on the technical SEO on your website.

There are other tools not directly related to technical SEO within Search Console. However, it is the one-stop shop for fixing most technical SEO issues as they pertain to Google directly. If your website were ever to receive a manual action penalty, Google would communicate with you through Search Console. Further, if you need to undergo the reconsideration review process, this is where that information is housed. Search Console is a powerful tool that, if mastered, ensures all the technical SEO checkboxes are ticked.

I want to briefly touch on how websites work. No, not the thousands of lines of code that make them load and function, but rather from thirty thousand feet. The reason I want to highlight each of these elements is to illustrate your need as a business owner to control your website. I have come across countless occasions where a website is being held hostage because a client gave them notice. You should always own your website, you should always own your URL, and you should know where the website is hosted. If you know these three things, you are in control of your web property.

URLs, Hosting, and Content Management Systems

Websites start with a basic URL. URLs come in all shapes and sizes. You may have seen some competitors that opted for a keyword-heavy URL (caraccidentlaw-yernow.com) or one that opted for a brand (GreenEllisLaw.com). Some have .com, some .net, some .gov, etc. Historically, having keywords in your website URL was a ranking factor.

> 📌 You should always own your website, you should always own your URL, and you should know where the website is hosted.

This, along with general vanity, is the reason some URLs cost $40,000 to include legal keywords. If you were able to purchase a domain with "injurylawyer" in it, you had a higher probability of ranking for that keyword. Back in the day, Google would even highlight the search term in the URL on the actual SERP. The power of having an exact-match URL is long gone. However, that is not to say it no longer matters.

The bottom line when picking a website URL is to stick with it. Constantly changing URLs, even through the proper implementation of redirects (which we will discuss in detail later), sets you back years from an SEO perspective. Google generally also does not like change. If you change your URL, you are introducing a new element to the SEO landscape that Google needs to assess and figure out what it is. No matter what, that takes time. Google can get confused, and rankings drops can result.

Additionally, there is a brand component to consider when switching URLs. Will consumers be confused by the new URL? Does it matter? Think about these questions and make sure you are confident in the answers before making a switch. It is critical that you stick with your URL, especially if you have invested thousands into moving it up in the rankings.

You purchase URLs at the registrar level. There are quite a few registrars out there; the most common is GoDaddy. Make sure you know what your GoDaddy or other registrar credentials are. Make sure the website is not set to private ownership. We want to be as transparent as possible with Google and the internet at large. Hiding our ownership information runs counter to that mission. Make sure that you have your URL secured for at least the next ten years. I have seen countless firms' websites go down because their credit card expired on GoDaddy.

In even more unfortunate cases, someone may purchase your expired domain at auction and try to sell it back to you for thousands of dollars. All of those situations can be avoided with proper maintenance and securing that URL for a significant period of time. After all, the cost is extremely minimal to prevent potentially catastrophic consequences.

You should also make sure you have access to your hosting account. Many agencies will have elite hosting packages with hosting providers, so it may not be in your best interest to host your own site. Furthermore, if something were to happen to the website, it would be fixed in a timelier manner if the website were hosted on the agency server. That being said, you absolutely should have access to your server build, which is where the website content management system (CMS) lives, and it is how the web page loads when someone hits your website URL.

The main website files are all housed on the hosting server. You may be thinking, *There are tons of hosts out there; how do I find the right one for me?* Well, keep an eye on speed and security. Many hosting companies have increased the security measures they take in recent years. Ask your hosting company what updates they have planned to address any security flaws that crop up. Finally, your website speed is greatly impacted by your hosting server performance. If your website is slow, consider taking steps at the server level to optimize the delivery of content, images, or specific code aspects.

Your hosting server is the place where your website CMS lives. Your CMS helps to deliver the pages you have written, images you have added, or videos you have made to the user in the way we all know and love. There are quite a few different CMSs out there. Some open-source CMSs include WordPress, Drupal, Joomla!, Magento, and Wix.

Some digital agencies will also create their own CMS. This can allow for the faster delivery of information or can serve as a way to lock you into a contract until the end of time. The key with a CMS is to know what you are on and understand how complex or easy it is to move. Many proprietary CMSs are notoriously difficult to move off of.

Consider web companies with proprietary CMS platforms—their clients live in a state of perpetual fear whenever they even consider moving. At BluShark, we build all of our websites on WordPress. It is the most common and widely used CMS out there, and we do that for multiple reasons, the primary one being that our clients own their own websites. If they want to move that website to another provider, we were so happy to have helped them on their path to internet marketing stardom, and we know we left that website in a better place than we found it.

You may have also heard of CMSs such as Wix and Squarespace. Clients who are just starting out or may be only a few years into their law firm ownership careers come to us frequently with websites on these CMSs. We always recommend a switch to WordPress. WordPress allows you to scale your website and the abilities that your website has. There are thousands of plugins and new ones coming out every day that help webmasters and marketers stay on the cutting edge from a technical perspective. WordPress is highly customizable—another reason it is our preferred CMS. Whenever choosing a CMS, pick the CMS for the future, not necessarily the CMS that you need right now.

> Whenever choosing a CMS, pick the CMS for the future, not necessarily the CMS that you need right now.

Speed Is Critical

A critical component of technical SEO is speed. When we refer to speed, we are referring to the speed at which a page loads across different devices and browsers. Different pages on a website may have different elements on them, and each of those elements contributes to how quickly a web page loads. At its core, speed comes down to how quickly data can be transferred from the server to the device a consumer holds in their hands.

To unpack page speed, you first need to understand what things slow down a website. We have all heard that large videos and images slow down websites, and this makes sense. The more elements a page has to load from the CMS, the longer it will take to do so. Do whatever you can to minimize the size of images and embed videos from YouTube for optimal video speed results.

Another very common reason websites are slow is that they are loading excessive scripts when a user first visits the website. Think about all the scripts you have running in the background: chat, retargeting Google, retargeting social, Google Analytics, call tracking, plus any number of other scripts coming from plugins that you may be running. These all have to load the first time a user visits the website, so keep this in mind and only leverage scripts that you need.

Further, use Google Tag Manager to house your scripts for even better results. Another reason websites can be slow is that they are sloppily coded or have excessive code on the page. This is a more difficult task to catch and manage, but if your Core Web Vitals (CWV) scores are consistently low, it may be time to have a second set of eyes review the coding on the page.

There are quite a few different tools out there that can help you measure your website's page speed. The most effective tool comes from Google itself. Originally, this tool was called the PageSpeed Insights tool; however, now it has evolved into the CWV tool. Google has stated that it will be updating the tool in time, but as of 2025, the tool measures loading, interactivity, and visual stability.

You may be thinking, *What the hell does that mean, and how does it apply to my website?* But Google outlines for us three distinct scores that provide us with some insight into what it and the consumer are experiencing when they come to your website.

The first of these elements is Largest Contentful Paint. This specific score measures loading performance, or how quickly elements are loading onto the page. The second is Interaction to Next Paint. This measures interactivity or how much time it takes from when a user initially lands on the website for the next visual element to load.

Finally, the tool looks at Cumulative Layout Shift (CLS). CLS measures how much the page layout moves around unexpectedly as it loads. An example of this is certain buttons that shift in the load process or images that shift around as the page is loading. What the CWV report gives you is insight into what specific aspect of your website is slow. *Is it how the images are loading or the images themselves?* By religiously running CWV tests, you will be able to proactively identify and address any speed issues that may come up.

One element of page speed that you should always keep in mind is that speed can fluctuate from device to device. You could have an incredibly fast desktop site, while the mobile site could be extremely slow. CWV allows you to see a report on both the desktop and mobile versions of your website, thereby highlighting any issues you have with either. CWV scores are also reported in Search Console, so if you are curious about your CWV, run the test or check that section of Search Console.

Different Approaches to Mobile Websites

There are different ways you can choose to deliver a mobile website. In today's world, most searches and website visits are conducted on mobile devices, so having a mobile website that delivers quickly and efficiently is extremely important.

Back when I started, you had to create a separate mobile website. You typically knew you were on one of these websites if there was an *m.* before the URL. These were mobile-specific websites or websites that were designed and built separately from their desktop counterparts. This is an important distinction, as m. websites are typically extremely customizable for the mobile environment.

These websites are difficult to maintain, as they have a completely separate code base that you are working off of. In addition, as referenced in the indexing section, m. websites will have different URLs than desktops. As a result, two separate site maps and two URLs (one for mobile and one for desktop) will be required for every page. Now, m. websites are fewer and farther between. Most websites utilize responsive designs, which are our preferred mobile website method.

Responsive designs are what the name says, and the website responds to the environment from which it was pulled up. This means that it is the same website for a desktop computer screen that is twenty-seven inches as it is for an iPhone. The same website design is delivered. It is simply resized or responds with a version of the website that is most applicable to your device. An easy way to test if your website is responsive is by taking a website view window and shrinking it. What happens? Does the formatting change? Does the header menu become a hamburger menu on the top right-hand corner? If yes, you have a responsive website.

Part of the beauty of responsive websites is that you don't have to do everything twice. You have one design for all devices. You have one set of URLs for Google to index, thus eliminating the possible confusion that could result, and when you update the website, you are updating it in two places at once. For these reasons, we feel strongly that responsive designs should be deployed whenever possible. They are the easiest design to maintain and are the easiest to rank.

The final type of mobile website we will be discussing is Accelerated Mobile Pages (AMP). The AMP project was started by Google back in 2015. The idea with AMP was to deliver content as quickly as possible to users. You may remember the lightning symbol on some mobile search results in the top right-hand corner that indicated the web page you were about to go to was an AMP page. AMP pages load extremely quickly because they are void of most heavy-loading elements. This means if you run AMP, you will be prohibited from the type of scripts you can run (for example, chat) or the visual elements that you can include on pages.

Many news organizations switched to AMP when it was released, and it made sense for them. News agencies are delivering tons of content to the general public on a daily basis. People want their news extremely quickly and may not hang out to read the entire story. AMP was made for this type of website, quite text-heavy without a need for visual elements.

AMP was not necessarily the answer for many law firms, as those visual elements and scripts directly contribute to mobile conversions. Eric Enge of Stone Temple Consulting did a fantastic case study on AMP. The conclusion of the study was that AMP did not significantly impact rankings for websites that had it. Further, without visual elements, conversions drop off, so keep this in mind if someone brings AMP to you as a solution to your technical SEO problems.

Be Willing to Change

One common reason people decide to stay with a provider that is no longer providing good service is that they are afraid their website traffic will nose-dive if they change anything. They may have had a previous experience where they lost rankings or traffic when they changed SEO vendors. When you switch vendors, many companies will change the fundamental structure of the website. They may change the structure of URLs, and when this occurs, it is critical that redirects are implemented properly.

With proper redirects, any link equity that existed on the previous URL should transfer. Additionally, and most importantly, you may have existing pages that are ranking. If you change URLs without implementing a redirect file, those ranking URLs will lead to a 404 error. This is a horrible user experience, and Google will soon knock you off the first page. Maintaining a redirect file, especially when multiple websites are involved, is critical to technical SEO success.

Google understands that from time to time, webmasters and business owners need to change the structure of their websites and URLs. As mentioned, redirects bring a user from an old URL to a new URL. When a successful 301 redirect is implemented, the user will be none the wiser that they went through a redirect.

Redirects are a fantastic way to maintain what you have, both rankings and equity, without always having to start again. However, redirect files themselves can be extremely temperamental. These files have to be checked and rechecked when a website changes hands. If there are 404 errors in the file or redirect loops, wherein a user is put in a never-ending cycle of redirects, this can cause serious SEO issues.

When implementing redirects, you should always do them one for one. This means that your old URL should point to the new URL. For example, xyz.com/dui-lawyer/ should redirect to xyz.com/dui/, xyz.com/assault-lawyer/ should redirect to xyz.com/assault/, and so on. You should not redirect all your old URLs to the home page. I have seen this done incorrectly hundreds of times. Redirects should always be one for one and should always bring the user to the next most relevant page.

An ideal redirect may take some content from the old page as a way of reinforcing the fact that this content has literally moved. Prepare your redirect file well in advance of a relaunch, and test every single redirect after the website is live. In one column, put the old URL. In another column, put the new URL. Keep track of this as you redo the website structure. Once it is live, click through every URL in the old URL column to ensure it matches up with the new URL you created. If everything checks out, you should be good to go.

Technical SEO Doesn't Have to Be Scary

Having a strong foundation is critical for SEO. Understanding what levers of that technical foundation you can pull to enhance page speed and other on-page SEO factors is critical. While technical SEO and development overall may seem daunting, if you can master the core concepts that relate to technical SEO, you will be able to provide a check on your SEO provider and continue to enhance your search engine visibility.

CHAPTER 8

STRUCTURE TO WIN

Twenty years ago, hiring a chief operating officer (COO) at a business-to-consumer law firm was practically unheard of. Law firms typically relied on receptionists or perhaps an office manager, but bringing on a highly compensated employee, who didn't directly generate billable hours, was considered unnecessary or even wasteful.

Today, however, this perspective severely limits the growth potential of many firms. I frequently encounter firm owners managing practices in the $1 million to $3 million revenue range who hit a growth ceiling simply because everything from client intake and marketing to HR management and their own legal caseload still funnels through them. This causes bottlenecks, overwhelming the firm owner with tasks that could and should be delegated.

I experienced this challenge firsthand at my own firm. Initially, I viewed hiring administrative or operations staff purely as an additional expense. It wasn't until we brought on skilled operations personnel that I realized these roles weren't just administrative overheads; they were critical investments in our firm's capacity to scale efficiently and sustainably.

In the same way that clear organizational structure and capable operations leadership allow your business to scale, a structured approach to your online presence similarly enhances your business's growth potential. Think of your website as the digital COO of your business. It should clearly communicate who you are, what you offer, and precisely whom you serve, eliminating confusion and maximizing efficiency.

You must leverage every tool at your disposal to educate search engines about your business clearly and effectively. Structured data, also known as Schema.org markup, is one of the most powerful tools available to achieve this clarity. Just as a COO organizes internal operations to boost productivity, structured data organizes your website's information to ensure it is efficiently processed and understood by search engines.

This chapter will guide you through the strategies and tools necessary to structure your digital presence effectively, ensuring both search engines and potential clients can clearly understand your value. We'll explore the role of structured data in enhancing visibility, credibility, and conversion rates, and discuss best practices for optimizing your local search presence to dominate the market and consistently win business.

Use Every Tool

Search marketers should use every tool at their disposal to educate the search engine about who they are, what they are selling, and whom they can help.

The more information the search engine has at its disposal, the more it will make use of that information. By utilizing this information, the search engine becomes slightly more predictable, allowing search marketers to continue optimizing and pushing better results to the top. One very effective way to deliver information to the search engine is through the use of structured data.

Structured data, or Schema.org markup, works behind the scenes of a website to inform the search engine crawlers about your website and your business. Certain forms of structured data also allow for information to be included about the business owner, can pull in information from third-party sources, and can even change the appearance of a website in the SERP. For all these reasons, you should be implementing structured data on your website.

Schema.org is a library of website code that you can implement on your website that, when properly executed, accomplishes its goal of communicating to the search engine what certain pages on your website are about. For our legal websites, we typically use at least four different structured data sets. Local business markup, attorney markup, review markup, and location markup are on most pages of our client's websites. Let's walk through these forms of markup to give you an idea of what each does.

Review markup is the most exciting of the bunch. It allows you to code reviews and star ratings on the backend of internal pages on your site. If done properly, and when Google decides it is cool, Google will show actual star ratings in the SERP. This is obviously a massive click-through rate boost if you are the only website on the first page in the organic listings that has a visible five-star rating. However, like most things with Google, lawyers took advantage of this form of markup, and Google has since cracked down on it when it is deployed. There are still active workarounds that search marketers can implement to try to get the star rating to show.

Another really cool form of markup is frequently asked questions (FAQs). You may have seen those organic listings that have those extra questions underneath them. That is done by FAQ markup.

You can enter the questions and answers that you want on the backend of the website. Unlike a reach snippet, this information is not necessarily directly on the page of content itself. It is markup running in the background of the page. If executed properly, and when Google chooses, you can see the questions appear underneath the organic listing on the SERP. This markup, mixed with review markup, gives you very valuable real estate on the first page and offers another click-through rate advantage when users are deciding between the first three listings.

Location markup simply tells the search engine where all your offices are located. Local markup helps us educate Google further that we are a local business in an area serving local people. Attorney markup allows you to tell Google that you are a lawyer. So, imagine the search engine crawler already knows your name, your business name, where your office is, that you are a lawyer, that your business is in the legal category, and even your hours of operation. Armed with that information, the search engine is able to accomplish a more concise and fuller picture of your business throughout the course of its crawl.

There is a tool, the Schema Markup Validator (https://validator.schema.org/), that lets you put your website URL through a scan to check if your markup is reading properly. In other words, it tests your markup to make sure all the necessary categories for that form of markup are fulfilled. Many forms of markup have multiple fields that need information properly entered and coded.

If you receive a warning during the scan, there is an issue with your markup. You need to check the code and make sure everything is entered properly. The great thing about this tool is that it will tell you what part of your markup is running into issues. It will also allow you to check your own structured data to see if the information is accurate. Having outdated markup is not good for you or your SEO.

The Value of Local Search

One of the ways we were able to scale Price Benowitz from three lawyers to over fifty is through the utilization of local search. When we started, we had three offices: one in DC, one in Maryland, and one in Virginia. Now, we have over twenty office locations. Part of the reason that local was such a strong component of our firm's growth strategy is that I saw the ROI.

By acquiring pins on the map, or additional office locations, I was seeing exponential returns, and a significant portion of that was due to local search. In this chapter, we will be diving deep into local search. We will be discussing how local search has evolved over the last ten years, how you can get started on local search, and which optimization techniques you can use to get better visibility. Furthermore, we will be examining the key conversion factors for local search, how users interact with local search, and where we anticipate local search will evolve in the future.

Local search, or as some commonly refer to it, "the map pack," shows underneath the paid ads but before the organic listings on the SERP. Additionally, it is what we are referring to when driving in your car and searching for something on Google Maps. The local search algorithm is different and distinct from the organic search algorithm. However, many of the signals that search engines look for are similar.

You may remember map packs of old that included seven listings. Originally, the local listings that appeared on the SERP had seven different business listings. This would obviously take up a big portion of the SERP, and at the time, LSAs were not a thing, so this map pack really dominated a lot of the first page. It made sense at the time; as Google was doubling down on its local product, it wanted to push users to the local listings more. However, with time, that began to change. Soon, the seven-pack became five and eventually what it is today, two or three.

This gradual loss of real estate did impact businesses that were generating a lot of business from local listings and were now outside of the top five, seven, or now three. Understanding what factors the local search algorithm was taking into consideration was critically important, especially as those factors changed with time or search marketers began optimizing for those signals. Like many things in SEO, staying on top of the changes that are occurring within each of the separate landscapes is paramount for success.

Build Your GBP

All things with local begin with your GBP. GBPs are like a virtual storefront for your business.

GBPs started as Google My Business (GMB) profiles back when Google+ was still a thing. For those of you too young to remember, Google+ was Google's attempt at social media. You could follow businesses, post content, like, comment, etc. At the time, some SEO specialists actually thought activity on Google+ correlated with higher local search rankings. Nevertheless, your GMB was your business profile within the Google+ platform. Now that Google+ is gone, GBPs have their own separate dashboard where you can create, manage, post, and view insights into the performance of your GBP.

Google has evolved the GBP quite a bit since the old days. GBPs now serve almost as a hub of user-generated information, as well as business-provided information, that people can come to and look at for more information about how you interact with your customers. Not only are your hours and address listed in the GBP, but people can also read reviews, view photos, look at common questions and answers, as well as look at popular times you are busy, visit your website, get directions, or connect with you on social media.

Your GBP not only serves as a place for people to find you but also as a place where people convert. We know that an educated user will check out your reviews to see if you have responded to any negative ones and may also view some questions and answers on your profile. Understand that your GBP serves as a conversion mechanism for potential clients to become clients. If your GBP is built out well and converts better than your competition, you will win the day and get more cases.

There are two possible scenarios in which you can get started with your GBP. The first is that you have been in business for some time but have yet to claim your GBP. Google is constantly crawling the internet, and even if you did not create a GBP, there is a chance that Google did so for you. This was not with malicious intent. Google more than likely crawled your website and found your business name, your phone number, your address, and other identifiable information and preloaded it into a Google Maps profile.

Now that this scraped profile exists, you need to claim that profile to take control of it and begin optimizing it for local search results. The other scenario is that you are creating a new address for a new office, or perhaps you already claimed your GBP but have not put any optimization efforts behind it. In both of these instances, if you sign into your Google account, you should be able to create a new location and prompt the verification for that office or make any necessary changes to your profile.

Not everyone can just sign onto Google and start creating listings. While this was the case ten years ago, Google got in some trouble over this back then, specifically with regard to some fake locksmith listings in New York. Now, Google takes steps to ensure that business listings that are listed on maps are legitimate. This all starts with the Google verification process, which has historically been an absolute nightmare.

Make Sure Your Business Is Verified

Verifying office locations on Google has evolved greatly over the years, especially as spam on Google Maps took off. Historically, to verify an office location, you had to prompt a postcard from Google that would arrive at the address you were trying to verify. This would include the suite number and the name of the business. If that card arrived, usually within two to three weeks, you would enter the personal identification number associated with the postcard to verify your listing. If it did not arrive in time, you could keep prompting postcards until that was no longer an option.

At that point, Google would request photo verification of the office. You would take photos of the office, send them over to Google, and eventually, it would confirm or deny the office as existing. This process has changed a great deal since. Now, often, there is no option to prompt a postcard at all. Photo verification has been replaced with video verification, wherein you literally walk around your office with the representative from Google on the phone. This is all in an effort to combat spam.

As spammers took over Google Maps, creating listings in parking lots and abandoned buildings, Google had to figure out a better way to crack down. In fact, there was even a story about how someone got an office verified in the White House. Because of this, Google was and still is extremely careful in the verification process.

The main takeaway when verifying a new office on Google is to have all your ducks in a row before you start the process. Google may request photos and a video. They may even ask for paperwork proof, all in an effort to prove that the office is, in fact, real. The more information you can provide to Google to show that the office location is real, the better off you will be.

If there are delays in getting this information to Google, not only does it look suspicious, but it also sets you back from a time perspective and will prohibit your growth. Google wants the office to be manned by someone, it wants to be able to see clients in the space, and it wants your signage visible. If you fulfill these criteria, you should be able to get your office verified.

There are instances in which a verified profile can become unverified, and you will have to go through the verification process again. Do your best to avoid having to go through verification repeatedly. Sometimes, this can be out of your control. For example, if you move offices or change the name of your business, there is a chance that Google will require you to reverify your business listing. You should make these moves with caution, although sometimes you can't avoid them when your lease comes to an end.

While your profile is being verified or once it is, you need to build out your GBP with as much information as possible. As noted earlier, your GBP is like a virtual storefront for your business. People can come here to look at photos, view your reviews, and even contact you. For this reason, apart from the optimization benefits it brings, you should always build out any available field you can in the GBP. Later, we will discuss GBP feature rollouts and the importance of staying on top of those, but for now, let's focus on your initial buildout.

Within your GBP, you should be able to add business information, a description, your hours of operation, photos, a menu, and product descriptions (if applicable); select a category; and set up messaging or an appointment link. Below, we will be highlighting a few critical elements of your GBP and why you should pay particular attention to some aspects of it rather than others.

One of the most important aspects of your GBP is your category. Your category tells Google at a very high level what your business is all about. Categories within GBP go relatively deep, depending on the practice area. For example, PI Attorney, Divorce Lawyer, Criminal Justice Attorney, and Immigration Lawyer are all categories you can pick from.

You can add multiple categories to a single GBP, but the one you select as your primary will carry more weight. Categories are one of the first things we audit for our clients. I can't tell you how many times I have seen a GBP with a category that was completely off. "Trial Lawyer" is a personal favorite of mine for PI lawyers. You may think of yourself as a litigator, but selecting that as a category when you are a PI attorney is a recipe for local SEO disaster.

Pay careful attention to the categories of your competition. If you are not ranking for a specific keyword, take note of the categories that are showing up well. Are they different? This is an easy way for you to check if you will be able to compete with these people on the local map.

A History of Local Updates

Like organic search, Google has launched quite a few updates to the local search algorithm as a means of creating a better user experience. Some of these updates were larger than others, but many were released with a better searcher experience in mind. As we discuss the local algorithm updates, try to identify any trends. You will see that, while Google doesn't tell us the direction it is taking locally, it sends us enough signals to interpret so that we can reasonably deduce what is coming next.

The first update that we should discuss is the **Bedlam update**. The Bedlam update is so-called because of the absolute chaos it caused. When Bedlam was first launched in 2019, mayhem erupted. No one could exactly pinpoint what was going on. We saw massive fluctuations in local search results.

With this update, Google showed us what it was trying to eliminate from the search results. In the update, businesses that were using executive office spaces, Regus suites, or WeWork suites were knocked out of the map pack, their listings suspended, and they were left to find another address.

The **Vicinity update** rolled out in 2021, and prior to its release, nothing had shaken up the local landscape more since Bedlam. Bedlam, one could argue, was done with good intentions, but the rollout itself was quite poor. Listings that should not have been impacted were suspended, and it took some time for things to settle back down. The Vicinity update was different. This update had one clear thing in mind: the user and their experience with the local three-pack.

The update was dubbed the Vicinity update because the biggest thing it impacted was how Google was weighing proximity in its local search algorithm.

This update shrunk the overall search radius that a local business could show up in. Before, even in competitive markets, you could have a single GBP show up across the city, even if the city was twenty square miles. There was an ability for an authoritative GBP to completely dominate a market. Vicinity completely changed that. What

Vicinity did was consider the point of search when determining whom to pull up in the local search results.

Vicinity opened our eyes to the direction that Google was moving in—a closer search result, one where proximity matters a great deal more than it ever had before. The local search world was reeling from the change, while Google was putting the user first. Let's think about this for a minute. Why would Google make this type of change? If you are in a city and you are looking for a coffee shop, and the result Google pulls up is fifteen miles from where you are—when you know there are three options within four blocks—it is not a good user experience. The same goes for a pizza place, a store, or a hair salon.

Google assumes that the closer a person is to a particular business, the more likely they are to frequent that business because it is close. Google deployed this method of thought across industries. What resulted was a completely altered map landscape and new factors you have to consider when deciding where to open a new office location.

From Reviews to Results

Local search has shifted to be one of the main mechanisms for conversion in digital marketing. The presence of reviews, in particular, gives potential customers insight into how a business conducts itself. This has given rise to more and more people looking to local search for answers to their problems. Local search is an extremely powerful way to generate new clients, so ensuring you are showing up as soon as possible in the map pack should remain a top digital priority.

CHAPTER 9

HOW TO RANK, EXPAND, AND DOMINATE LOCAL SEARCH

O pening a new office location is one of the most powerful ways to grow your law firm and expand your reach in local search. But it's also one of the easiest places to go wrong if you're not careful. As we've seen, Google doesn't treat every new office equally. It's not just about having a physical space. It's about having the *right* kind of space in the *right* place, one that helps your local SEO instead of hurting it.

The truth is, plenty of well-intentioned firms sign leases in locations that ultimately hurt their visibility online. Maybe it's a shared executive office that Google flags as spammy. Maybe it's a building already saturated with competing law firms in the same category. Or maybe the new office doesn't extend your search radius at all and ends up overlapping with your existing footprint.

Before you rush into expansion, it's critical to take a step back and evaluate whether the location you're eyeing will actually move the needle in local rankings. Getting this right means doing your homework—not just on foot traffic or square footage, but on how Google views that address and what digital potential it carries.

In this chapter, we'll break down exactly how to vet a new office location from an SEO perspective. From scanning the address for red flags to analyzing existing GBP listings nearby, these steps will help ensure your new location is positioned for success—both physically and digitally. Here are a few places to start.

First, run Google searches on the potential address you picked and see what shows up. Do ads for Regis or executive office spaces come up? If so, you have a problem.

Next, run the address through Google and see what other businesses have GBPs in the building. If a firm with the same practice area as you is already in the building, you will encounter a filter, so make sure you are the only one in that GBP category located at that address.

Finally, make sure this is in a population center. As we just learned, proximity and vicinity to the searcher are now critical ranking factors. We want to make sure the address gives us an additional search radius. We don't want to open an office that overlaps with the radius of an existing location.

There may be more opportunities in other areas of a city that you should pursue. Consider all of these factors the next time you think about opening an office. The last thing you want to do is sign a lease for an address that doesn't set you up for success.

Optimizing for Local Rankings

Every year, there are studies published on the main local search ranking factors. One such study published by Whitespark surveyed local search marketers on what they saw as some of the biggest ranking factors for local search. This list is quite accurate when pinpointing the main ranking factors for local search. We will walk through the top-ranking factors and what you can do to optimize your GBP for them.

The first and most important ranking factor is your primary GBP category. As we discussed when setting up your GBP, the selection of this category is critical to how Google views your business as a whole. If you select the wrong category during this process, you will have serious issues with ranking. Understand these categories, and again, make sure you are staying on top of new categories as they come out. The list of possible legal categories has expanded a great deal in the last five years alone. Make sure you always have your primary category set to the practice area that keeps the lights on at your firm.

The second-ranking factor that we should take a moment to discuss is the utilization of keywords in your business name. Using keywords in your business name is an optimization technique that works. If you want to be found for car accidents, calling yourself the "XYZ" car accident lawyer gives you a better chance of ranking higher more quickly for the search "car accident lawyer" or even "accident lawyer."

You may be sitting there thinking, *Wait a second, didn't they have an update that caused a bunch of chaos because people were spamming business names with keywords?*

You would be correct; you can't simply add keywords to your business name without due consideration. However, as lawyers, filing a "doing business as" (DBA) with your secretary of state will help you comply with Google's guidelines, ensuring your listed business name matches your registered name while still allowing you to incorporate keywords. It's important to note that we don't recommend frequently changing your business name based on varying circumstances. Choose the most universal terms possible while ensuring you don't deter potential clients, and you will improve your local visibility rankings.

Here is a checklist of all attributes in the GBP backend:

- GBP information
    - About
        - → Name
        - → Category
        - → Description
        - → Opening date
        - → Phone number (+ tracking number)
        - → Website (+ tracking URL)
        - → Social profiles
    - Location
        - → Address
        - → Service areas
        - → Hours
    - Attributes
        - → Owner info
        - → Accessibility
        - → Amenities
        - → Parking

- → Planning

- → Service options

- → Languages

- ▫ Reviews

  - → Review responses

- ▫ Products

- ▫ Services

- ▫ Booking link

- ▫ Q&A

- ▫ GBP posts

Other Ranking Factors to Consider

The next few ranking factors are relatively self-explanatory. One, the **proximity** of the local business to the searcher, we already discussed in great detail. We know from the Vicinity update that proximity to the searcher is extremely important, and if there are other businesses closer to the searcher with similar authority, they will most likely show up first.

The next, having an **address** in the city where a search is being conducted may seem relatively unimportant, but it is extremely consequential for local search. What this ranking factor means is that if your address, as seen on Google, is listed in city name *A*, you will not rank in city name *B*. In some cities, the boundaries of where one town ends and another begins are quite blurred, so it is important to base this on what Google is insisting the cities are, not what your address from USPS may say. I have come across countless examples where friends have asked me to recommend local search fixes, only to find they want to rank in a city they don't have an office in. In this scenario, usually the only solution is to go find a new office in the city you do want to show up in.

Another key local ranking factor centers around **user-generated content**, in this case, reviews. Reviews are extremely important for local rankings. If you have significantly fewer reviews than the competition, you will have a hard time moving up the local rankings. Further, review counts are a conversion factor. If you have 150 reviews and the other people have 40, you will get the phone calls.

Some of the most effective review outreach campaigns come from your staff. Since they communicate with potential clients and clients frequently, they may have an existing relationship with the client. Play to the client's comfort when making the ask and follow-up. Don't be afraid to push for reviews. More reviews will directly correlate to more cases for your firm.

Additionally, it is important to note that the words used in reviews do matter. If you have reviews that are keyword heavy, Google understands and picks up on that. It will move you up in the local rankings if those reviews are positive and include keywords. For your favorite client, perhaps ask them to leave a review specifically stating the type of case they had. Including the words *car accident* in the review is extremely powerful.

One thing that we have deployed for our BluShark clients is calling people to ask for reviews. When you do a text or email outreach campaign for reviews, the response rate is 1 to 2 percent. So, if you have one hundred people, you get one review. That is not a high enough conversion rate when some firms only handle twenty cases at a time. By calling people and asking them for reviews, that rate ticks up to 12 to 20 percent. This greatly increases the likelihood that someone will leave you a review and will increase your local rankings.

Focus on Quality

Many of the signals that help websites rank well organically also help them rank well locally. The local algorithm still takes into consideration website authority signals when determining whom to show in the three-pack. Firms that have fully built-out GBPs but terrible websites will have a hard time ranking in even semi-competitive markets, so coupling an organic with a local strategy will help you generate a higher ROI. When you set up your GBP, you will need to enter a website URL, and the website URL you enter carries weight with how Google views you locally. It will crawl that website URL and pick up on any signals you may have left behind. What are those website signals that Google appreciates? Here are some ways for you to optimize your website for better local search results.

First, if you localize your content, especially for the URL you list on your GBP, you will help Google understand where you are and for what terms you want to be found. Including the "geo + keyword" formula in your content will help to optimize that content for local search. Having the location name of your office in the title tag, the meta description, and a heading helps send signals to Google that you are where you are and that you want to be found for what you do.

Additionally, internal links, especially to internal practice area pages that are not performing well in local search, do wonders. Making sure to follow internal linking best practices discussed in the on-page SEO chapter of this book and including the city name in the anchor text of those internal links will help Google understand you want to be found for those terms. Keep this in mind when you are publishing your next page of content or are struggling with local rankings for a particular keyword.

Another key component to local rankings is the overall authority of your website and, more importantly, the URL that is linked in your GBP. We build authority for the website through link building and healthy traffic to the website. If you have a link-building strategy in place that encompasses building authority links from a diverse group of sources, then you are in great shape. In addition, if you have multiple offices, you will need to think about building authority to all the URLs listed on your GBPs, or they will not perform. In other words, each office location should have an individualized link-building strategy that builds authority to the page you list in the GBP.

If you fail to build authority for one, it will have a hard time ranking. The overall authority of the website will be taken into consideration, but the URL you list on your GBP should also have a decent amount of authority built into it. Be extremely careful, but one way to move the local rankings even further is by using exact-match anchor text on a few sparing external links that include the location you want to be found in. Again, these links need to be natural, and keywords with locations in them are historically clunky, but if you can find an opportunity to do this, you should seize it. Authority building as it pertains to local SEO is yet another example where the organic and local algorithms work in tandem to deliver the best possible result to the searcher.

Leverage New GBP Features

Google is constantly coming out with new features for GBPs. When we refer to GBP features, we are referring to the additional fields in the GBP backend that Google allows business owners or consumers to take advantage of. Some GBP features we have already discussed include reviews, Q&As, and others. We recommend that you take advantage of any new GBP feature that rolls out. Google usually deploys these intentionally, and you should take advantage of any opportunity you have to message your clients. Below, we will discuss and review a few of these features to give you an idea of how you should be leveraging them.

One feature that gives businesses another opportunity to communicate with potential clients is through GBP posts. GBP posts appear on your GBP profile, and you could think of these almost as an opportunity for you to highlight a specific practice area, offers or promotions, or any other brand differentiator. This is not an opportunity for you to spam the posts section with keywords you want to be found for.

Another important GBP feature is responding to reviews. As we discussed earlier in this chapter, reviews are a ranking factor. The number you have and the words that are used in the reviews are important local ranking factors. Responding to those reviews is an important best practice you should be following at your business and is another feature of the GBP.

Many educated consumers will view your review responses, especially your responses to negative reviews, as a way to see how you interact with clients in good times and in bad. Take care to respond to reviews. Make sure you personalize the responses. There is nothing worse than coming to a GBP where all the review responses are the exact same. It looks like the business doesn't care about its customers.

Be sure to stay on top of any new features that are rolling out on GBP. These features may contribute to local rankings, local conversions, or both. Understand and take the time to build out these sections of your GBP with as much information as possible.

Remember, this is another opportunity for you to communicate with potential clients. Seize that moment and increase the number of leads you are generating for your business.

NAPs and Local Citations

Historically, one important local ranking factor was the existence of local citations and the consistency of your name, address, and phone number (NAP) on those local directories. Local directories exist as a way for people to find businesses outside of the search engine. Not unlike GBPs, many allow you to create a profile, build it out in a similar manner to GBPs, and generate traffic and a link from these citations.

Google, of course, crawls these local citations and the information contained therein. Historically, if you had the most local citations, along with a few other ranking factors, you would show up high on local searches. This changed many years ago, and local citations started to fall by the wayside. But it is important for you to understand the history of local citations, how they played a role in the local algorithm, and why you should consider using them moving forward, even if their benefit has diminished a great deal.

It is important not only for Google's purposes but also for your overall customer experience to ensure your name, address, phone number, and website (NAPW) are critical components of your digital identity. You need to protect these components as much as possible, ensuring that they are consistent across all third-party websites. Google doesn't like to be confused, and even though the search engine has gotten significantly smarter, leaving any room for error can be concerning.

Additionally, you want users to see your brand unified across the internet. You don't need potential or current customers calling phone numbers that are old, going to old office addresses, or referring to your business by the wrong name. How will that future referral go? Keeping your NAPW consistent is a basic component of local SEO, even if the consequences are not as bad as they used to be.

Finally, professional and legal directories also play a role in citations and NAP consistency. Legal directories typically require you to enter your NAPW when you are creating a profile. Google will crawl these legal directories and associate the listing with your brand. Further, legal directories are extremely topical. You are a lawyer. Of course, you should have your NAP plastered on as many legal directories as you can find. The more we educate the search bot about who you are and what you want to be found for, the more likely that is to occur.

The key takeaway with NAPW and local citations is that while their power has diminished over time, it is important to have a consistent NAP and as many local citations as possible. Remember, Google is constantly crawling the internet, picking up on all the signals you, as a search marketer, are attempting to send it. The more positive, consistent signals that you can send to them about your brand, the more successful your local SEO campaign will be.

Stay on Top of New Local Tools

There is a wide array of local tools you can use to optimize and keep track of your local campaigns and rankings. Below, we will discuss some of our favorite local tools and how you can implement them for your local SEO campaign.

Our favorite tool for keeping track of local rankings is **Local Viking**. What Local Viking does is run geo-grids for your keywords around your office location. These scans are essentially searches from points around your office location. You can set the radius around your office for where you want those searches to run.

After the Vicinity update, Local Viking continues to be very important to helping you understand your local search reach radius. These grids show you where you have rankings and where you have room for improvement. These grids also help you identify potential opportunities for future office locations. Local Viking is not the only tool that runs geo-grids. Local Falcon and Places Scout are two other very effective tools for running geo-grids and tracking local rankings.

BrightLocal is a citation-building service, but along with quite a few others, such as Moz, Whitespark, and Semrush, it also offers citation management services. This means that when you need to make a change to your address, your DBA finally goes through, and you need to change your name or your phone number changes, you can make all these adjustments within these services.

In other words, these tools are one-stop shops for listing management. This helps to maintain consistency across the web and allows you to quickly adapt should the need arise. Further, many of these tools will directly connect with your GBP. This allows you to make your change in the tool dashboard instead of having to log in to your GBP.

Stay on top of new tools and local service trends by following the Local Search Forum. This forum, run by a fantastic local SEO company, Sterling Sky, is a place where local search marketers can go and discuss any issues they are running into, successes they are having, or overall fluctuations that are occurring throughout the local search. We highly recommend you start following these forums, as the landscape of local search is constantly changing.

Why You Should Have a Multi-Office Strategy

With all its local updates, Google has had the user experience in mind. Some were released as a way to combat local spam, which was prevalent and contaminating the search results. Others were geared toward enhancing the user experience by shrinking the map and taking the point of search or proximity into serious consideration. In theory, this was to improve user experience and present results that were closer to the person searching. It is our estimation that this trend will continue, and it is one reason we continue to recommend to our clients a multi-office strategy.

As local competition grows, Google's local search tools will continue to get more competitive. The more pins that you put on the map, the more opportunities you will have to appear in local three-packs. Remember that your ability to take one office and dominate local search is gone. Depending on the market size and competitiveness, you need to be strategically thinking about where pins should go on the map to maximize your ROI.

When the Vicinity update was launched, firms that had multiple offices were much better off. Their risk was diversified so that if they lost reach in one market, they had other markets to make up for it. Further, the point of search is critically important now. We think that Google will continue to move in this direction. That means that the more pins you can put on the map, the higher the likelihood you will be next to someone who is conducting a search.

Moreover, adding additional office locations gives you access to a new customer base. As we previously discussed, you are not going to rank locally in a city in which you do not have an office location. As you max out the search reach radius you get from your first office location, expanding into new markets with another office location will keep your growth on track, so long as it is done intentionally and strategically.

Another recent trend we have seen in the local search arena is the gradual shift in user behavior toward local search. Historically, we would get a decent amount of traffic and conversions from both organic and local searches. In 2023 and 2024, we noticed a shift in where conversions were coming from on the search engines. Across multiple markets, we saw organic conversions or calls from organic clicks drop. However, they were being replaced sometimes by more than 20 to 30 percent with local conversions or calls.

This shift partially makes sense. As GBPs are providing even more information for an educated consumer to consider, searchers are checking locally before making that buying decision. It will be very interesting to see if this trend continues. If it does, the importance of local search and optimizing your local presence for conversions will only increase.

Another reason I think it is so important to continue to find additional office opportunities is the intersection of generative AI and local search. As generative AI gets more sophisticated, there is a chance that people will absorb information in a different way. They may not be visiting your website to learn about the statute of limitations; they may be asking a chatbot. However, when it comes to making a buying decision, we firmly believe that consumers will still consider local search when deciding to pick up the phone and call.

AI doesn't show reviews, at least not right now. It doesn't provide you with photos to humanize the experience or see how a business responds to negative feedback. People will still want that human confirmation that the decision they are making is good and true. For this reason, you should continue to think about your local footprint and take the time to build a strong local SEO strategy.

Don't Put Off Ranking

Now that you have the components of local search, get started. Claim your GBP if you haven't done so already, and get to work optimizing the profile. Start adding photos, launch a review campaign, and don't forget the core components of SEO that help you rank locally, too. Start planning your next office and start generating leads from local search.

CHAPTER 10

THE SCIENCE OF PAID SEARCH

n previous chapters, we have discussed the overall importance of having as much visibility as possible on the first page of the search results. Paid search ads show up above the organic and local results. This means that firms listed in the paid ads section of Google are seen first by users on mobile and desktop devices. An example can be seen on the next page.

Skilled DC DUI Attorney | Price Benowitz LLP | criminallawdc.com

Ad www.criminallawdc.com/dui ⌄

Our **lawyers** are ready to fight for you. Call today! No obligation. Sat/Sun Consults Offered. Former Prosecutors. Call or Chat Open 24/7. Types: DUI, Fraud, Federal Charges, Assault, Sex Crimes.

D.C. Criminal Law Lawyer - smithlaw.net

Ad www.smithlaw.net/ ⌄ (301) 555-7777

Protect Yourself. Know Your Rights. Speak To A **Criminal Lawyer** Today. 37 Years Of Experience. Free Legal Consultation. Highlights: Over 37 Years Of Experience, Free & Confidential Initial Consultations.

📍 5555 Search Dr, Rockville, MD

Contact Us in Arlington County | Tough Criminal Charge Defense

Ad defense.abclaw.com/ ⌄

We'll Go Above & Beyond to Protect Your Rights & Future. Call for a Free Consult. Cost-Effective Counsel. Boutique **Law** Firm. Locally Known Firm. Client-Centered Counsel. Skilled Trial Attorney. DUI Defense · Felony Charges · Misdemeanors · Defense Services · Arrested? · White Collar Crimes

Best DWI Attorney 2017 | Defense Team Response 24/7

Ad www.johnlawyer.com/ ⌄

High Client Reviews/Payment Plans Tailored to Your Case/ Fmr Prosecutor on Staff. Weekends-Attorney OnCall. Free Consultations. Types: DWI/DUI **Defense**, OWI & POCA **Defense**, Felony & Misd. **Defense**.

We want users to see your firm listing as many times as we can to increase the probability of a click and eventual conversion. This is why it is so important to have an organic, local, and paid strategy, in which each element complements the others. One way that a firm can influence the amount of visibility that it has on the first page is through the utilization of paid ads.

Remember that Google is in the business of making money on clicks. Its highest revenue source is from what it makes with paid ads. This means it is constantly trying to find more ways to get people to click on paid ads placements. This has resulted in many new opportunities for paid search advertisers to take up additional real estate on the first page.

There are many great components of paid ads. The first and most obvious is that you can buy your way to the top very expeditiously. With organic and local search, it takes time to get a website and GBP listing to the top three positions. By utilizing the different components of paid search, one can increase their visibility on the first page while waiting for the organic and local results to kick in.

Understand KPIs and Track Conversions

We will dive into the different forms of paid search advertising shortly. However, it is worth noting that another huge component of paid search is the ability for advertisers to select the specific keywords that they want to show up for. In other words, say a firm is specifically looking for medical malpractice cases in which a medical device was left inside an individual's body. This is a highly specific case type. Paid ads will allow a law firm to specifically target the search term "lawyer for medical malpractice device in the body" while not targeting medical malpractice cases more generally. It is critical that you maintain and run a strong paid campaign that focuses on refining keywords so that you are continually targeting the cases that you want.

If you choose to run a paid search campaign, it is critical that you understand the key performance indicators (KPIs) for your campaign and have a system for tracking conversions. Paid search allows for one of the clearest ROI calculations that a firm can do. It is critical for your firm to analyze the results of specific marketing campaigns.

One of the biggest pitfalls I see law firms fall victim to is that they don't understand the ROI that they are getting from their different marketing channels. With paid search, and when

> If you choose to run a paid search campaign, it is critical that you understand the key performance indicators (KPIs) for your campaign and have a system for tracking conversions.

proper tracking is implemented, you can track the life cycle of a click or a call all the way from beginning to end. It is a clear cost per click, cost per lead, and eventual cost per case.

Another important thing to consider is the history of paid ads. **Paid ads**, at their core, are an auction system. What this means is that whoever is willing to pay the most for a keyword is most likely to be in the top spot on the first page. Market pressures can drive the costs of certain keywords up over time, making your future ROI smaller and smaller.

With paid ads, there is a threshold beyond which the campaign no longer sees the same type of ROI. If you are seeing success, sometimes spending more does not necessarily equate to a higher ROI. In other words, there is a breaking point where your budget and potential lead quantity collide.

Find the Sweet Spot

The key to any paid campaign is to find that sweet spot. Understand how much you need to spend in order to maximize your return. In some instances, this means starting with a budget of, for example, $4,000. After the first two weeks, you run through your budget, get good calls, and sign up some cases. You raise the budget to $6,500—that trend continues. You raise the budget to $10,000, assuming that you will continue the trend of good calls and cases.

However, that extra $3,500 is not bringing in the quality of case you want. Your declines are up, and your ROI is lower than when the spend was at $6,500. In this example, the ideal budget is $6,500, as that breaking point of a true ROI was reached. This is why it is critical to continually monitor and test your campaigns. Paid campaigns are extremely temperamental, so when running tests, understand your variables and track everything accordingly.

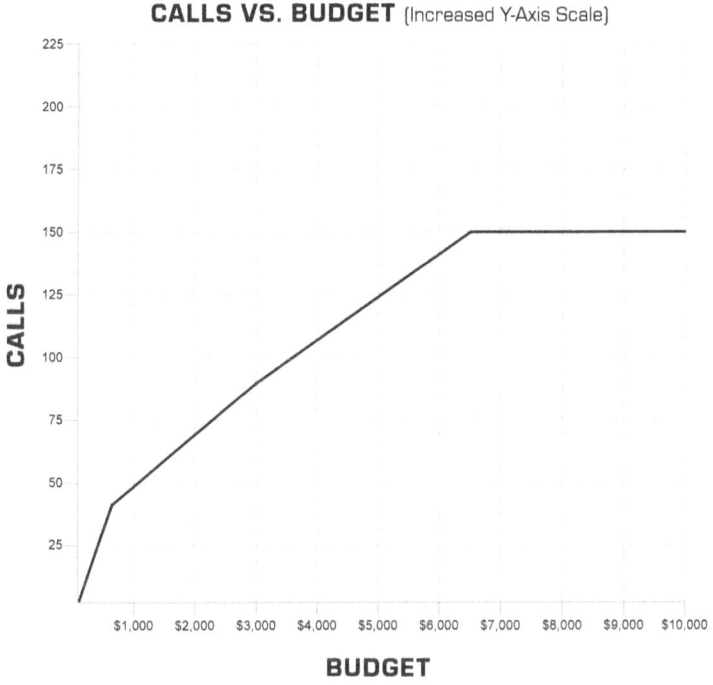

Testing is critical for a successful paid campaign. There are many different components to each type of paid ad, and each component plays a role in the overall success of the ad. Additionally, Google is constantly coming out with new automated features that, in theory, help to optimize a business's ad campaign. Features such as automated bidding, responsive ads, and automated optimizations for conversions are all examples of the features being rolled out to help a business owner run a more effective campaign.

With these and any other new Google rollout, we say, "Trust, but verify." It is important to test new features when they drop to see if they do help your campaign. For some paid campaigns in some markets, we have seen ridiculous success with responsive ads and setting a campaign to optimize conversions. In other markets, we have seen the opposite.

Many clients often ask me how long it takes before they see some results from a paid search. Many think that paid search is like a faucet. You turn it on, and all the leads start flowing out. Unfortunately, that could not be further from the truth. Paid ads campaigns take time to see success.

Most importantly, paid ads campaigns, if managed properly, learn over time and become more successful. Later, we will discuss the importance of keywords and negative keywords for optimizing your paid campaign, but your keywords will be much more targeted after the first ninety days than when you start a campaign. After ninety days, you will have data on what search queries people are actually searching, so then you can refine your keywords even more. You will have data on what ads are performing better than others, so you can further refine and optimize your ad copy.

You will have better bid data so that you can optimize your bids to show where you want to show. We typically tell our clients to let paid ads campaigns run for ninety days, so we have all the data in front of us to make the best decision for the future of their law firm. It should be noted that, in some markets, it does not make sense to run paid ads. There are some markets where it clicks.

Paid ads campaigns are temperamental. Making changes haphazardly and frequently will lead to a drop-off in campaign performance. As mentioned previously, these campaigns do learn as they progress, so if you are constantly making changes, it is difficult for Google to even learn from you what you are trying to do. We will discuss in detail the different types of search campaigns and the complexities that arise from each later on.

Different Types of Paid Search

Google offers search marketers different forms of paid ads. We will be discussing traditional PPC ads, LSAs, retargeting ads, and display network ads. We will be discussing these types of ads all within the Google platform, although the information discussed regarding PPC ads can also be used for Bing.

Google continues to push its traditional PPC advertising as much as possible. This makes sense, as it has led to it becoming a multi-billion-dollar company with unlimited future potential. With that in mind, the traditional PPC advertising platform is understandably complex and well developed. This method of Google advertising has by far the most features rolled out for search marketers to use.

That being said, many people are competing within the Google search ads platform, so how do you make your law firm stand out? How do you become number one? How do you know when paid search is maybe not the right marketing channel for you in your market?

The first thing to know about Google PPC ads is that they are run through Google Ads. Google Ads is Google's one-stop shop for finding keywords, creating ads, tracking clicks, and ultimately running the campaign. Google Ads has gone through multiple iterations throughout the years. With each iteration comes new features and new data. Every time a new rollout drops, which is not all that frequent, we focus on understanding the new features and reporting.

Is there any new piece of data that we could not access before that can now help to better optimize our campaign? Are there any new automations that have rolled out that we should test? Finally, how is AI understanding the data within the platform, if at all? Ultimately, we want to find out how we can better leverage Google Ads data to understand and deliver a better message to our customers.

Traditional search PPC is run through an auction structure. That auction is based on keywords and the specific match types you choose for those keywords. To understand a budget and begin to spec out a campaign, you need to build a keyword list.

Building a Keyword List

When starting a PPC campaign, I always recommend that people start with a list of keywords that they create. You should have a basic understanding of the types of keywords that your potential clients are searching for. Do this before working with different tools.

In fact, do this exercise: List out all the questions that you get during an intake or even throughout the beginning part of a case. What words do all these questions have in common? Take all these words and phrases and put them in a spreadsheet. Now add "lawyer/ attorney + your location" to the beginning or end of those common phrases. What did you find?

Now that you have a keyword list based on what you think people are searching for, check to see the actual search volumes for your keywords and locate additional keywords that your customers may also be searching for. Within Google Ads, there is a tool called the Keyword Planner. The Keyword Planner allows someone to enter search terms such as "car accident lawyer" and see how many projected monthly searches that keyword will get. The Keyword Planner also gives you an estimated top-of-page bid, or the estimated cost it will take to be on the top of the first page per click.

The Keyword Planner will also allow you to expand your keyword list to include the terms needed for a successful campaign. This is easier said than done. You will have to utilize the tool to find similar keywords or phrases that also receive decent search volume. The more you dig, the more you may find opportunities. The legal industry for search PPC is hypercompetitive. The more you expand and dig into potential keyword options, the higher the likelihood that you come across a bucket of keywords that are much cheaper than the money keywords "car accident lawyer."

Do not solely rely on the Keyword Planner for building your keyword list. It is essential to utilize other tools to identify the most effective keywords for your target market. SpyFu is a wonderful tool that gives insights into a market. It includes competitor analysis so you can understand the ads that you will be competing against. Take caution with any third-party budget predictors (and even the keyword planner). Most of these budget predictors are aggregating historical data, which means they are typically off by a high enough margin of error that some would say they are not worth much.

Your goal with the keyword list should be to determine if you have the right combination of search volume for your keywords and estimate cost. I have seen many campaigns flail in the wind because there was not enough search volume to generate enough clicks and, in turn, phone calls. If you are not generating enough clicks because your keyword list is not large enough or you are limited by geographic reach, it is a recipe for disaster. The goal is to find that sweet spot where you have the right keywords targeting enough of the right people. Once you have that keyword list and a rough estimate of searches and cost per search, you can begin to formulate a budget.

Understanding the Auction Platform

Building a budget within the Google Ads platform may be seen as that mountain you don't want to climb. However, it is not as difficult as it sounds. As mentioned previously, traditional Google PPC runs on an auction platform. You are bidding on placement for your ads for specific search terms.

The bids that you select in Google Ads for a specific keyword are priced per click. The price per click on keywords in various industries varies greatly over time, and because it is an auction platform, it is critical that you stay on top of the price per click for each of your search terms in your campaigns. I remember one example from fourteen years ago, when my marketing person (not Brenton) set a bid for a keyword in a small Virginia town to automated bidding.

When she started the campaign, the cost per click was around $15 a click. After nine months, in that same small town, through automated bidding, the click was running at $115 a click. Since Google Ads is an auction platform, competition picked up in that specific market; most likely, a small local player decided to give Google PPC a shot. Over the course of those nine months, a bidding war ensued for our same keyword.

Since automated bidding was set, the war continued until it hit that peak of $115. At that point, we were burning through our budget with no success because we were not paying attention to the auction in this market. This story should illustrate the importance of monitoring the cost per click for each keyword in your campaign.

There is no better way to understand what a good budget is than to run campaigns, look at the data, and continue to test. However, many firms do not have the luxury of testing through hundreds of thousands of dollars to find the right budget, the right keywords, the right geographic area, and the right ads. A well-paid agency will be able to work with you on these questions to find that budget sweet spot.

The biggest mistake that we see people make with campaign budgets is not setting them large enough. This industry is highly competitive, and in certain markets, entering with a low budget and low bids will yield poor clicks and low-quality calls. The money will be spent, but it will be wasted.

Building Paid Campaigns

Now that you have an idea of the budget and a list of keywords, it is time to start building your campaign. First, though, it is important to understand the campaign setup hierarchy within Google Ads. At each level of the hierarchy, you can control different campaign parameters. By understanding the hierarchy, you can organize your keywords in a way that sets you up for success.

> The biggest mistake that we see people make with campaign budgets is not setting them large enough.

At the top level, you have your campaign. At the campaign level, you can set your budget and geographic targeting parameters. If you are running multiple campaigns that have different budgets and are targeting different geographic areas, you will want to set up multiple campaigns. For example, let's say you are an employment law PI practice. Those practices have different marketing budgets, and your PI lawyer only takes cases in the southwest part of the state. In this example, you would want to set up two campaigns, one for PI targeting the southwest part of the state and another for employment law targeting the entire state.

The next level is the ad group level. It is at this level where you set up your keywords and set bids for those keywords. It is at this level that you will be doing the most customization. If, for example, you are setting up a PI campaign targeting most types of PI cases, your ad groups may be set up something like this:

- Ad group 1: car accident

- Ad group 2: truck accident

- Ad group 3: motorcycle accident

- Ad group 4: bus accident

- Ad group 5: slip and fall accident

Each of these ad groups is going to have a specific set of keywords, and those keywords or keyword phrases should not overlap. The more specific you get with the keywords you use in your ad groups, the more flexibility and customization you will have with the ads you are running.

The final tier on the hierarchy is the ad level itself. It is at this level where you will set your ad copy, ad headlines, and landing page URLs and choose which ads to run per ad group. This is why it is so important to set up the different ad groups by keyword category. You will be able to customize the ads and ad copy to correspond to the relevant keyword group.

In other words, you can set "Ad group 1: car accident" to run ads to your specific car accident landing page URL. You can include words like "car accident lawyer" in your headline and in your ad copy to provide the best possible user experience. This matters a great deal as we dive into the other components of a traditional Google paid ads campaign.

It is important to set up your ads campaign following best practices for keyword types so that you can easily change things in a timely manner. The more you break down your campaigns, the more you can individually customize how each campaign is performing. When building your paid ads campaign keyword list, consider starting with the keywords you have already created for organic search. Like many things in SEO, we don't want to reinvent the wheel.

Don't Take Your Eye off the Ball

To run a successful paid search campaign, you need to closely monitor your ROI, budget, and ads. Taking your eyes off any of these components can end up costing you. Choosing the wrong keywords can also be a costly mistake, so don't be afraid to leverage tools such as Keyword Planner and SpyFu to inform your PPC keyword strategy. Constantly testing and fine-tuning your strategy to find your budget sweet spot can help ensure your firm stands out without wasting money.

CHAPTER 11

LANDING CLIENTS, NOT JUST CLICKS

After developing your keyword list, getting an estimated budget, and seeing the estimated search volume for those keywords, it is time to enter those keywords at the ad group level into your campaign. Understanding the different keyword match types in Google is critically important for executing a strong campaign.

Additionally, there is a direct cost associated with each match type used in the auction system on Google Ads, meaning that certain match types may cost more than others. Further, different match types will absolutely bring different types of clicks and, in turn, users to your site. The key is to understand which types of keyword matches bring in the most relevant and most likely to buy clicks.

There are three main match types that you can use when setting your campaign keywords in Google. The first is broad match.

Broad Match

With broad-match search, ads may show on searches related to your keyword. This is the broadest way to target searches through Google Ads (hence the name).

For example, continuing to use "Ad group 1: car accident" from the previous section, if you set your keywords to "car accident lawyer" using broad match, your ad may show on a search for "How long will my accident case take?" Now, on the surface, this may not immediately raise the alarm for you; however, someone searching may very well already have a case with a lawyer. They are just generally searching for information about timetables for settlements in accidents like theirs.

If you factor in that click, it may be forty to sixty dollars. Is that a risk you are willing to take? Broad match should be leveraged when search volume is very low or the results of the other match types are not meeting expectations. When utilizing broad match, it is critical to have a well-kept negative keyword list, which we will discuss in greater detail later. To enter a keyword using broad match, simply type the keyword with no modifiers.

Phrase Match

The next keyword match type is phrase match. With phrase match, ads may show on searches that may include the meaning of your word. The key here is the word *include*. The fact that your ads can show up when a phrase that includes your keyword is mentioned is what sets phrase match apart.

For example, utilizing the same keywords in the example above, if someone were to search "How much does an accident attorney cost?" your ad may appear. Again, the meaning of your original keyword car accident lawyer is captured within the phrase *How much does*.

Exact Match

Exact match is another match type that Google Ads uses when determining which ads to display. Exact-match ads show on searches that are the same as your keyword. For example, in the example above, someone searching for a car accident lawyer would see our ad appear if we were using the exact-match type. Exact match is typically quite a bit more expensive than broad match. Why? Generally, more people are bidding on those exact-match terms, and there is less inventory of searches for those exact-match terms. This drives the cost up, so keep a close eye on the exact-match campaign cost per click, as there may be cheaper ways to achieve the same outcome.

Modified Broad Matching

I would be remiss if I did not mention modified broad matching (mod broad). Mod broads allow you as a search marketer to target a broader audience while still making sure your keyword is included. In other words, you would be able to capture the "car accident lawyer near me" search mentioned in the example above by utilizing a mod broad of "+car +accident +lawyer." Those + symbols mean that so long as those words are included in the broad-match search, your ad may show up. Keep this in mind when building out a campaign and leveraging the different keyword match types that are available to you.

How to Use Negative Keywords

Even with a stellar match-type strategy, things can come completely undone without the proper utilization of negative keywords. Within Google Ads, Google allows you to set a list of keywords that, if searched, will cause your ad to not appear. In other words, if someone searches a word you know is a non-revenue-generating keyword, you can ensure your ad does not show up, and you do not pay for that click. We all know the potential criminal defense client who has called every law firm in your market looking for the answer that doesn't exist—the retainer is free.

That potential client almost certainly searched with the words *free* or *cheap*. If you had utilized negative keywords properly, you would have prevented your ad from ever showing to this person and maybe avoided the call altogether. Further, you would not have had to pay for that click, ultimately saving your marketing dollars for a potential client click that will convert.

Negative keyword lists should be continually refined and updated. At BluShark, we have a negative keyword list that is deployed strategically across paid client accounts that number nearly fifty thousand. You may be thinking, *That sounds like a lot; what if I don't have the time or money to develop that sort of list?*

Start with what you know. Develop your own negative keyword list based on triggers that you know are cases you will not take. Talk with your intake team and gather some information on the reasons you recently turned down cases. Are there any commonalities there with specific words or phrases that people use? If you can drill down on the terms by focusing on the data, you can develop a robust negative keyword list that will end up saving you thousands of dollars long-term.

A campaign should always start with some negative keywords. Even Morgan & Morgan says no to some cases. However, once you have a campaign up and running, a quick and easy way to continually build out your negative keyword list is by checking the actual search terms you are paying for already. Within Google Ads, you can view the search terms or previous searches people entered to arrive and ultimately click on your ad. There will always be some unwanted clicks in there, especially at the beginning of a campaign. The most important thing is to learn and adapt from those errant clicks.

Add certain words or even full phrases to your negative keyword list. This type of search term check should be performed daily to ensure you are catching any keywords that may have slipped through the cracks. Further, there may be some gold hiding in that search term list. Maybe there are long-tail keywords that you can start to include in an ad group that has a low cost per click and lower than average cost per case. Keeping an up-to-date negative keyword list and having a process to keep that list updated is critical for strong campaign performance.

Use Ad Copy to Fuel Your Campaign

Strong campaign performance is also fueled by ad copy that resonates with the user and, most importantly, gets them to take that all-important next action—clicking. There are parameters for the number of characters that you can use in your ad headline and in your ad copy. There are many factors that you should consider when writing your ad copy.

The first and most important consideration is what keyword you are targeting. Your keywords are set into different ad groups, and for each ad group, we can and should have multiple ads that are running. Let's take the same example of "Ad group 1: car accident." Since our keywords are targeting the car accident category (this would include terms such as "car accident lawyer," "car accident attorney," "car accident lawyer near me," etc.), we would want to tailor our ad copy to a searcher using those search terms.

When anyone is searching for something on Google, there are few greater feelings than absolutely nailing a search. When the exact words that you used are in the headings, you see those same words in the meta description and feel a sense of self-affirmation: *Damn, I am good at Googling stuff.* You, as a search marketer, should use that same psychology when writing your ad copy for your ad groups.

If someone is searching "car accident lawyer," I would hope part of your heading for the ad and ad copy itself (the words that appear underneath the ad) include the words "car accident lawyer." If an ad shows up with ad copy and a headline that says "bike accident lawyer," that user, who is clearly looking for a car accident lawyer, will not click on your ad. It may be difficult to capture every possible variation of the search term that you have. However, you can set different ads per keyword group—meaning that you do not need to create different ads for variations on the words *lawyer* and *attorney* or *accident* and *crash accident.*

Those terms are similar enough that a user should be able to understand that the service is the same. However, if you have another keyword, such as "car accident lawyer near me," and your ad copy specifically mentions your local affiliations, those types of connections can go a long way with users. Ensuring that your ad copy and headline have some form of the keywords you are targeting is critical for ad copy success.

Landing Pages

When talking about traditional PPC ads, we also need to consider that generating the click is half the battle. Once the searcher has landed on your website, the real work begins to turn that click into a call and, eventually, a client. Landing pages are critical for the success of traditional PPC campaigns. There has been a long history of squeeze page best practices since the early days of selling things on the internet; however, there are some basics that anyone running a PPC campaign should consider for their landing page.

> The click is half the battle. Once the searcher has landed on your website, the real work begins to turn that click into a call and, eventually, a client.

In theory, your ad educated the user about what they were about to land on. Hopefully, it included the keywords that they searched for and enticed them enough to find out more about who you are and what you do. Your landing page should include the keyword(s) and relevant common variations of those keywords. The landing page should include some copy that educates the user about the next step in the process. It may answer some common questions that people in their circumstances need to know.

We don't want to include a wall of text, especially on mobile phones. That is not fun to read, and people will bounce right off the page. Instead, we need to balance the important visual elements, sell our firm, and provide the user with the information they were looking for. Calls to action throughout the landing page, be they forms, chats, or a phone number, that scroll with you as you scroll down the page are also critical so the user takes that necessary next step of contacting the firm.

Of course, the basic technical elements need to exist on this landing page as well. If it is slow, people will bounce right off the page and click on the next ad. If it looks great on desktop but half the elements are missing on mobile, that is going to lead to conversion issues. After all, you are paying for the traffic that is coming to these pages. You must have the technical fundamentals in place, or it will be even more challenging to get a positive ROI.

Tracking on your landing pages is also important for gauging campaign success. A/B testing your landing pages is a great way to learn which elements of a landing page are working better than others. This includes call tracking, Google Analytics, form tracking, and any other conversion tracking you want in place (for example, a conversion for someone staying on the site for a certain period of time).

There are many different conversion tracking metrics that you can pick from. We recommend at least the basics: call tracking, forms, chat, and Google Analytics. You want to know what types of traffic are landing on the site. For example, if your overall traffic is up, but your calls and forms are not up, and you are wondering what is going on, there is a potential conversion issue there.

On the other hand, if your traffic is down and calls and forms are the same, perhaps you have an ad copy and click-through rate issue that needs to be addressed. Thinking about PPC in this light will help you understand the different levers that you can pull when optimizing a campaign.

Search Impression Share

Search impression share (SIS) is one of my favorite metrics that Google Ads reports on. SIS calculates your rough percentage of overall ad market share for a specific set of keywords. Think of this metric as airtime for TV commercials. There are only a certain number of fifteen-, thirty-, and sixty-second spots available. This percentage can guide you on how much airtime you are taking up.

In the paid search arena, if this percentage is low, at 45 percent, it means that there is a lot of opportunity for you to expand your reach and possible share of impressions for a given set of keywords. This would mean either expanding your budget and bids for the keywords you have or building out your keyword list to include more relevant terms in addition to the terms you are already bidding on.

Now, let's say your SIS was at 98 percent for a keyword set, and you wanted to keep expanding your practice. Increasing your budget on your existing keywords is not going to move the needle much. In this instance, we would either need to increase the number of keywords that you are targeting to reach new people or expand the geographic reach of your campaign to try to reach new markets.

SIS is a great metric to look at when analyzing growth opportunities that may exist on the PPC frontier. Lower SISs usually mean there is an opportunity for a campaign to grow or be better optimized for a better ROI.

Ad Extensions and Bid Adjustments

Ad extensions are another way you can better optimize your ad to not only increase clicks but also take up more real estate on the top of the first page of Google. There are many different types of ad extensions that a business can utilize. Some examples include review extensions, location extensions, sitelink extensions, social extensions, callout extensions, and many others.

What these extensions do is provide the user with additional opportunities to learn more about your business. It also gives the business owner the opportunity to provide more useful information to the user, to hopefully get them to take the next step and contact the business. On the next page is a useful example of ad extensions.

You will notice from this example that the review extension allows for the paid search marketer to include relevant reviews, awards, and accolades. Please note that this is not applicable to all business types, including law firms. Sitelink extensions provide the searcher with additional opportunities to go to different pages on our website. Maybe they are looking to meet the team immediately, or they already know they want to hit the contact page. With sitelink extensions, users can immediately click on those links instead of clicking on the landing page link and navigating to the page of their choosing. Social extensions allow you to connect applicable social platforms to your ad campaign.

Google is also rolling out new extensions that are intended to meet users where they are at the moment. There is no better example of this than with contact forms and message extensions. With both of these extensions, Google is telling us it understands that the way people are contacting businesses has changed. Users no longer have to place a phone call to a firm to get help. In fact, many people prefer contacting businesses through online messages or text. By enabling these additional contact extensions, you are providing the user with additional opportunities to reach out to you in the manner that is most convenient and comfortable for them.

Finally, the most important type of ad extension, and one every law firm should be running, is location extensions. Adding location extensions to your ad allows for a connection with your GBP. That means that the information from your GBP will be pulled to the bottom of your ad. Additionally, this is how you get your ad listed in local search/maps. While Google is currently experimenting with adding LSAs to local search, equipping the location extension will allow for your ad to show at the top of the three-pack. Below is an example of location extensions in action:

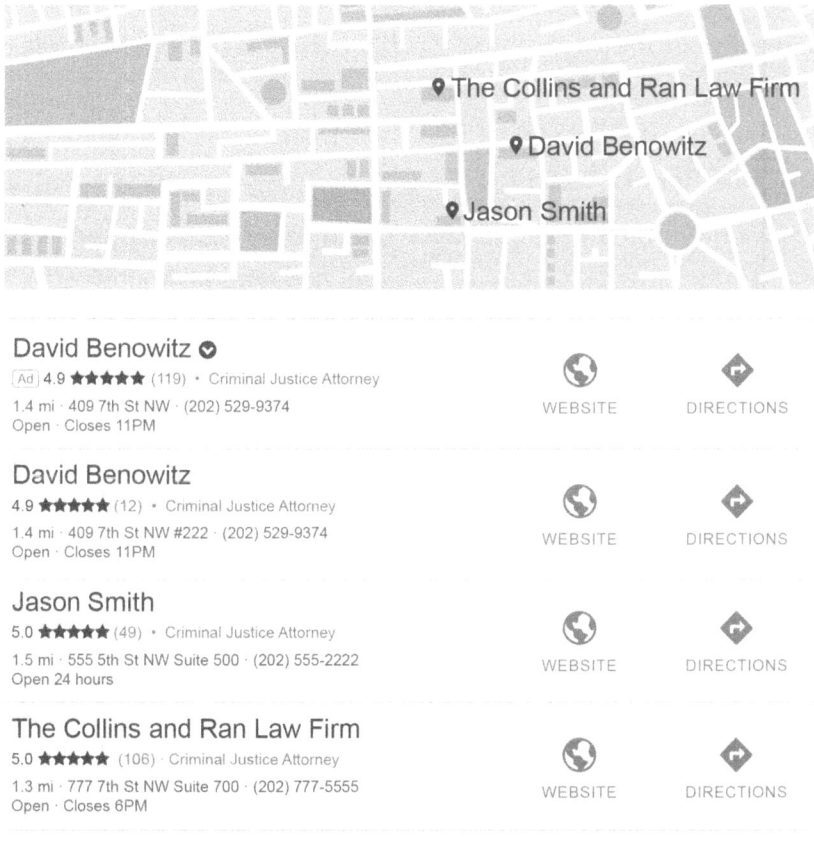

It should be noted that it is ultimately up to Google to decide whether or not to display any of these extensions. The best we can do is understand all the different extensions that are available to us and choose the best possible ones for our potential clients.

Another thing to consider when building out your PPC campaign is what types of devices your potential clients are searching for you on and when. Within the Google Ads platform, you can set specific bid adjustments that correspond to certain points in the day (time of day) and even mobile versus desktop devices. If you think most of your potential clients are finding you on a mobile phone, increase that bid adjustment for mobile and see what happens. Like all the other tests we mentioned previously, it is critical that you have proper tracking and a process for determining whether a test was successful or not.

PPC Made Easy

The world of traditional PPC may sound daunting, but it isn't with the right partner and an understanding that data fuels all decision-making. Paid campaigns are extremely ROI driven. Unlike organic and local search, we have a lot more information on the users who come to us through paid clicks. Because of this, you must leverage that information to understand if your paid campaigns are working for or against you.

CHAPTER 12

LSAS AND THE FUTURE OF PAID SEARCH

W hen people ask why we have a futurist in residence, my immediate response is: "Why don't *you*?" Leading Price Benowitz LLP and BluShark Digital has taught me the importance of anticipating changes and preparing proactively for the future, particularly in rapidly evolving fields such as digital marketing and paid search. Many businesses become so absorbed in daily operations that they lose sight of emerging opportunities and potential disruptions that lie just ahead.

A few years ago, we recognized the need for a dedicated role focused on future trends and challenges. Someone who could help us stay ahead rather than simply keep pace. Thus, the role of futurist in residence was created, and Peter Shankman became the obvious choice.

Peter's career has been marked by innovation. After his early days at AOL, he founded Help a Reporter Out, which was successfully acquired. He's also built and sold other successful ventures and authored multiple books, and he has a proven record of identifying trends before they become mainstream. Bitcoin and virtual real estate are notable examples.

Having Peter on board allows us to look further down the road than most businesses. In the world of paid search, where strategies and technologies evolve rapidly, maintaining a future-focused perspective is not just beneficial but essential.

One of the newest and most impactful innovations we've encountered in paid search is Google's introduction of LSAs. LSAs fundamentally alter the way businesses connect with customers by enabling direct contact from the search results page, bypassing the traditional click-to-website approach. This new format, where businesses pay per lead rather than per click, significantly changes the dynamic of paid advertising.

In this chapter, we'll explore the importance of understanding and embracing new trends such as LSAs, along with insights into their history, setup, optimization, and future potential. By staying proactive and adaptive, you'll ensure your business remains ahead of competitors and fully leverages opportunities provided by emerging technologies in paid search.

The History of LSAs

LSAs are intended to provide the user with an opportunity to connect with a business directly without ever leaving the SERP. The biggest difference between LSAs and traditional PPC or display advertising is that with LSAs, a business is paying per call instead of per click. This has revolutionized the Google paid arena.

No longer does a business have to worry about converting a click to a call once it lands on your website. Instead, a user can click your ad and either call or message your business directly, without ever leaving the SERP or visiting your website.

Another reason that LSAs are so impactful is their placement on the search engine. Currently, three LSAs appear above the paid search results.

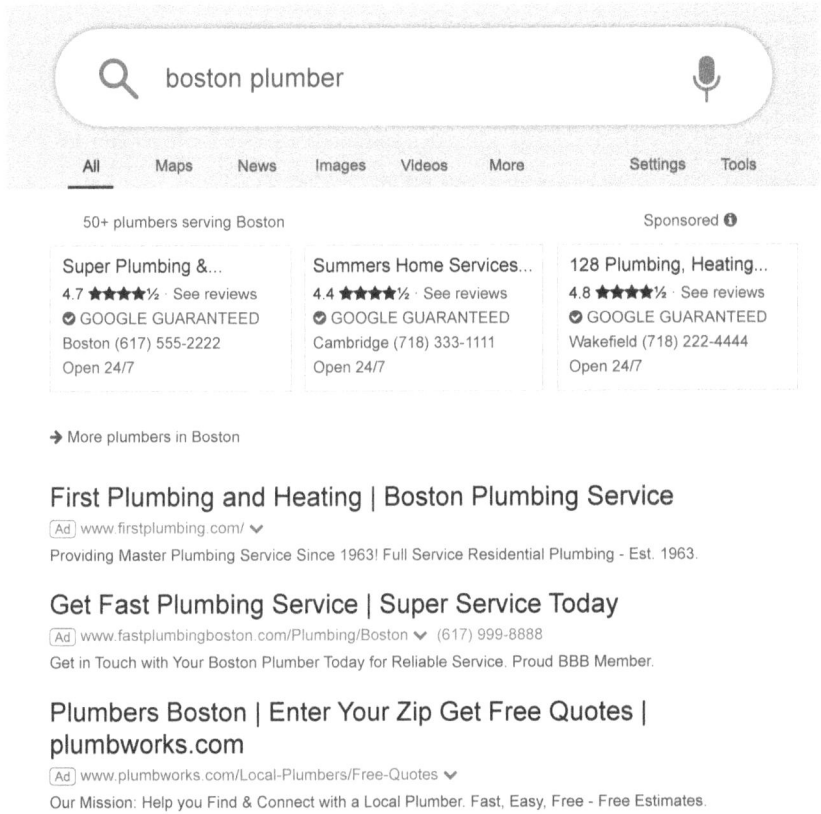

This is prime real estate on the first page of Google, and as mentioned in previous chapters, another opportunity for potential customers to see your brand and business on the first page. We know that the more touchpoints users have with us on the first page, the more likely they are to click and convert to a client.

LSAs were initially introduced to the search engine in 2020 and initially started in the home services industry. Like most things that Google rolls out, they started slowly in a few markets and industries and gradually expanded to more. When LSAs came to the legal industry, it was a slow rollout, first hitting a few markets on the West Coast in the family law industry and eventually rolling out to most legal verticals across the country.

LSAs, at their core, are a lead generation service. These ads show up first on the SERP, and the ad itself is different from other ads on Google. This is part of the appeal of LSAs. The ads themselves are displayed in a manner that conveys trust and authority for the businesses running these ads. One reason for this is the Google Screened badge that appears on a local service ad profile.

When starting a local service ad account, you will be required to submit certain information in order to get this Google Screened badge, hook up your GBP to your account, and get your account active. Google requires a business owner to submit their bar license and proof of insurance, along with their personal information for a background check.

It should be noted that the background check process itself has changed over time. At first, background checks were required for any business running LSAs. The background checks were intended to be conducted on any individual at the servicing business who would interact with the customers. After the first eight months, this requirement went away.

As of May 2024, Google has rolled back out the background check verification step. Even accounts that currently have live LSAs will need to submit and fulfill the background check requirement. We still recommend that only the business owner complete this step, but the background check process has caused serious issues in the past simply because the service Google uses to conduct these checks was overburdened or lacked support, and the process itself was extremely glitchy.

LSAs also carry a level of authority and trust not only because of the Google Screened badge but also because of the appearance of a review count and star rating that is displayed. Many customers today are looking to user-generated information to learn about a business and find out more about past interactions it has had with the public. Reviews are the best source of information for this.

An educated user is going to look at the review total and overall rating before making a buying decision. Most will also look at the reviews themselves, locate any negative reviews, and see how you, as a business owner, responded in a tough time. Reviews carry an extra degree of legitimacy and weight in the user's eye. Google chose to show LSAs with reviews to reinforce their authenticity to the user.

LSAs also include a headshot, years in business, hours of operation, and a contact phone number. That headshot, again, is intended to drive home a degree of authenticity. It introduces imagery to the SERP that doesn't exist through any other Google ad format, thereby making it stand out above the other paid, local, and organic listings. The hours of operation are intended to provide the user with a sense of immediacy and urgency. *The business is here to solve your problem right now with the touch of a button; just give them a call.* Additionally, the years in business provide the user with some understanding of the business's experience handling a case like theirs, all without the user ever leaving the SERP. All of these factors are meant to encourage users to click on LSAs, and by most accounts, it does seem to be working.

When LSAs began rolling out to the legal industry, it was anything but smooth. There were a series of relatively serious glitches that search marketers had to contend with throughout the rollout. Issues would occur in which submitted data to Google would no longer show as submitted, causing delays in getting ads live. In another example, there was a glitch across multiple LSA accounts that was causing review counts on the LSA profiles to be drastically off.

We had a client who had been in practice for over twenty years, and after their LSA went live, it showed the practice had been in business for three years. These were all glitches with the LSA platform, and this is yet another example of Google's iffy rollouts of new products. It is critical that you pay extra close attention to campaign performance with any new Google product. If no one had checked the aforementioned profiles that had glitches, it could have been weeks or months before the issues were resolved. Having a process and an individual responsible for your LSA campaign is critical for the campaign to be successful.

Getting Started with LSAs

LSAs are a fantastic way to get your feet wet in the Google paid search arena. We almost always recommend to our clients that they start their paid search budget on LSA. That is due to the nature of these paid campaigns. You are paying by the lead instead of by the click or impression. We are able to track these calls and figure out what is monetized for your firm in a relatively quick and easy manner.

There are fewer hoops to go through in terms of actually getting the campaign live. You don't need a landing page, ad copy, or all the other core elements of a strong paid advertising campaign that we have discussed in previous chapters. LSAs are an easy way to see if a paid search may be right for you and your business.

The LSA dashboard is located within the Google Ads platform. There is a separate section for LSAs that you can click on to view any active LSA campaigns, pending campaigns, etc. It is here that you will begin entering the necessary information Google requires for any active LSA campaign. After your personal information is entered, it will take some time for the campaign to go live (anywhere from forty-eight hours to two weeks).

Since we are dealing with Google here, it can be difficult to expedite this process. In addition, if a background check is required, you are now working with a third party to continue to process an LSA application. Keep this in mind when you are thinking about launching an LSA campaign. Starting early will give you a head start to counter any unforeseen delays.

Once your personal information is submitted, the next step is to hook your account up to your GBP. Your GBP plays a huge role in determining how successful your LSA campaign is going to be. There is not a separate buildout for an LSA; you are leveraging the already created GBP that is active for your business. If you do not have an active GBP to use, you will not be able to run LSA.

It is critical that you optimize your GBP as much as possible before starting an LSA campaign. This should not prevent you from running an LSA campaign. However, the more your GBP is optimized for success, the more likely you are to see success running LSAs. Additionally, we always recommend that when running LSA, you have messaging turned on. This is a big ranking factor that we will be discussing later in the chapter. However, it is best to set up messaging and create a process for answering messages as early as possible.

Now that we have all of the information submitted and our GBP hooked up to our LSA account, once everything is approved by Google, we must select in what geographic areas we want our ads to appear, to whom, and when. LSAs are unlike search PPC in many ways, so nailing the setup can be critical for overall campaign success.

LSAs are run differently from traditional PPC in that you are not specifically bidding on keywords in a traditional auction sense. Instead, you select an overall category and relevant subcategories that you want leads for, and Google determines when to show your ads for relevant searches. Current categories for legal include criminal law, estate law, malpractice law, business law, disability law, family law, PI law, traffic law, DUI law, litigation law, malpractice law, and real estate law. There are a few other niche categories as well, but these give you an overall sense of the type of legal categories you must select from.

Almost Ready for Launch

At this point, your campaign is almost ready for launch. You need to set a budget and see how far that takes you. Budget setting in LSAs can be difficult. Without an understanding of how LSAs perform overall, setting the wrong budget or not optimizing your budget for better ad placement can lead to disaster.

First, you need to understand how LSA leads are charged. LSAs are charged on a per-call basis. That means if someone clicks your ad and literally calls or messages your business, at that point, you are charged. The budget forecasting available within the LSA platform is extremely weak, so you need to rely on historical campaign performance when coming up with a budget. Usually, we like to start with a minimum budget of at least $1,000 a week for a PI LSA.

Keep in mind that each call or message can range in cost from $180 to $400, so this minimum budget allows for at least three to five calls per week. Without a budget minimum of at least $4,000, competing and having a successful campaign will be extremely difficult. Depending on the market, this minimum may not be high enough, so once you start getting cost-per-call data, figure out what the right balance is.

Currently, there is automated or manual bidding within Google that you can set. These bids are per call, not per search, so keep that in mind. We have found that Google's automated bidding performs significantly better than manual bidding. Since the LSA platform is relatively antiquated compared to the complex auction platform that is traditional PPC, relying on automated bidding has proved fruitful, given that Google controls so many of the levers that dictate which LSAs show for what searches.

We have seen countless campaigns come to us with extremely low minimum budgets, wrong categories selected, inactive hours of operation, and very poor performance. Poor performance in the LSA world means that your ad is not getting phone calls, is showing up for the wrong searches, or is generating the wrong type of leads. By prioritizing the optimization of these LSAs, a business can see success, but it requires a detail-oriented perspective.

LSA Ranking Factors

As we discussed, LSAs are directly tied to your GBP. If you lack reviews on your GBP to begin with, you almost certainly will have a difficult time competing in the LSA frontier. Reviews are so important to Google that there is also a separate link you can use to build reviews specifically on your LSA profile. We have run case studies to see if building reviews to the LSA links boosts ad ranking. However, our results were inconclusive.

Reviews are a critical ranking factor for LSAs and even more so when a user is deciding whether or not to call your business. If someone sees a list of businesses, they almost certainly will not call the one with the lowest number of reviews. As a conversion mechanism, it is important to keep pace with your competition on the review front. It is especially important for the LSA campaign's success.

Another important ranking factor for LSA campaigns is your budget and, more specifically, how you structure your budget within the LSA platform. One thing we have learned about LSAs is that the platform is not super sophisticated. One way for you to optimize your ad position is to inflate your weekly budget artificially. You can do this up to, as of July 2024, $1.4 million.

There is no way on earth you will ever spend that much in one week, especially if you have someone watching and monitoring campaign performance. Google wants businesses to spend money on LSAs. They are even egalitarian to a certain extent in how they go about distributing the leads. They will mix in firms that you may think of as smaller players, those with very low review counts or with low budgets, as a means of giving them a taste of what it's like to get paid leads. If we tell Google we are willing to spend the maximum weekly budget, it seems to think that we deserve more leads. Thus, we end up with better ad rank and more phone calls and leads.

Once you do hit your weekly budget, bring the budget back down to where you want it. This mechanism for optimizing LSAs will not be around forever. As the platform gets more sophisticated, this type of artificial budgeting will no longer work. However, since there are a few optimization levers that we can pull at this time, we must take advantage of any opportunity that may present itself. Often overlooked but critically important, another ranking factor is responsiveness.

Finally, test your LSA message leads. Understand that this is a hot lead that needs to be dealt with urgently. If you have messaging on, you will rank higher, but if those messages are left unanswered, your responsiveness will take a hit. Find and fix these holes in your intake before you run LSAs. If you get put in the doghouse for responsiveness, it can be extremely difficult to get back out.

One ranking factor that is now most likely going away is over-disputing. With the removal of the manual dispute process, this is most likely no longer a ranking factor. However, it is important to discuss as it directly plays a role in how Google thinks about lead distribution overall.

The Future of LSAs

One of the most exciting parts of being a search marketer is the constantly changing world that we live in. Search engines are always coming up with new products or ways to leverage existing products that, in the end, help drive new customers to our businesses. LSAs are relatively new in terms of their lifetime on the search engine. They release, tweak, adapt, and evolve the platform every day.

As LSAs are deployed to local map packs, they are highlighting the local nature of the ad even more. We believe that, eventually, the location of the searcher will become a very important LSA ranking factor, just as it has been with local search. When that time comes, running a multi-office strategy will be the most successful, as you will have more opportunities to be close to the original point of search. Thinking ahead, it is best for you as a business owner to continue to open more office locations. The more pins that are on the map, the more opportunities there are for you to capture a wider swath of potential search traffic.

With all these predictions, the underlying theme is that LSAs will continue to get more competitive and will continue to get more expensive. It is critical that you have a multichannel marketing strategy so that, when the day comes when LSAs are no longer a net positive in your market, you are protected. You have a local and organic strategy in place and may also have some nuanced traditional PPC campaigns that you are ready to deploy.

You need to be working with a partner who understands the overall ethos of Google and its direction for the future, as well as what it is doing now to maximize the return you can get from your LSA campaign. Now that you know what LSAs are, how they work, how to launch a campaign, and what to look out for when a campaign is live, what are you waiting for? LSAs are a great way to get started with Google paid advertising, so give them a shot. See what leads they bring, and continue to think about new tactics to grow your business.

AI and the Future of Paid Search

It's clear that AI is dramatically reshaping so much, including the world of paid search. It's transforming everything from ad targeting and bidding strategies to performance analysis and customer engagement. Platforms such as Google Ads now leverage sophisticated AI-driven algorithms—such as Smart Bidding and responsive search ads—to better understand user intent, optimize ad delivery, and maximize ROI. Gone are the days of manually adjusting bids based purely on keywords. Today's success in paid search hinges on intelligently crafted campaigns that effectively meet user expectations and behaviors.

One significant advantage of AI in paid search is its unparalleled ability to provide deep insights into consumer behavior. AI-powered analytics tools quickly process vast amounts of data, uncovering trends, patterns, and valuable insights into user preferences. This helps you tailor your paid campaigns more precisely, ensuring ads appear to the right audiences at optimal times. Instead of relying solely on intuition, you can now make informed, data-driven decisions.

AI also significantly streamlines the creative aspect of paid search campaigns. Automated tools can generate dynamic ad copy, adapt headlines, and optimize calls to action in real time, making it easier and quicker to run highly effective campaigns. While human creativity remains essential, AI greatly enhances productivity and scalability, enabling businesses to rapidly test and refine multiple ad variations without substantially increasing their workloads.

From a technical standpoint, AI simplifies routine paid search tasks such as keyword research, audience segmentation, budget allocation, and performance monitoring. By automating these repetitive yet crucial activities, marketers can focus more strategically on campaign innovation, audience targeting, and creative experimentation.

Last, AI has revolutionized the way marketers measure, predict, and optimize paid search performance. Through predictive analytics and advanced forecasting models, businesses can now anticipate changes in user behavior, adjust campaigns proactively, and quickly respond to shifts in market conditions. This agility helps marketers maintain a competitive edge and sustain visibility in a rapidly evolving digital advertising landscape. Simply put, AI is making paid search smarter, faster, and considerably more strategic.

What Does This Mean?

So what does this mean for you as a reader? With paid search evolving rapidly through the rise of innovations such as AI-powered bidding strategies, responsive search ads, and LSAs, staying competitive now requires quick, thoughtful adaptation. The expansion of LSAs and other emerging paid search features underscores the importance of agility and readiness to embrace and leverage new advertising channels and technologies effectively.

Adapting does not mean discarding strategies that have worked in the past. Instead, it involves strategically integrating new tools and AI-driven practices to complement your existing paid search strengths. Successfully utilizing features such as LSAs and Smart Bidding demands a deep understanding of Google's continually evolving platform and the ability to capitalize on its advanced capabilities. Similarly, embracing AI to enhance paid search strategies doesn't replace human judgment; rather, it enriches your capacity to anticipate consumer needs, deliver personalized experiences, and optimize advertising efficiency.

> Adapting does not mean discarding strategies that have worked in the past. Instead, it involves strategically integrating new tools and AI-driven practices to complement your existing paid search strengths.

Ultimately, the businesses poised to thrive in this dynamic environment are those willing to continually experiment, learn, and pivot swiftly when needed. Investing in understanding these emerging trends positions your business for sustainable, long-term success. Adaptability will become your greatest asset, enabling your campaigns to stay highly targeted, effective, and profitable in the face of rapid technological advances and shifting consumer behaviors.

So embrace these innovations with a proactive mindset. Whether you're mastering LSAs or harnessing the advanced analytics and optimization capabilities offered by AI, your willingness to adapt and evolve will define your future success. The paid search arena is dynamic, challenging, and full of opportunity, and it's *yours* to shape.

TWO STEPS YOU CAN TAKE TODAY

As we have discussed throughout the course of this book, it is critical that you track your SEO and other digital campaigns. Tracking has gotten more advanced with time, and understanding the KPIs of your SEO campaign along with calculating your ROI should be monthly exercises your firm is conducting. Truth be told, most firms are not.

Most firms are unaware of which marketing channels are working for them and which ones are costing them money. Successfully tracking and understanding the metrics of your SEO campaign will allow you to make more educated decisions about where to spend your hard-earned marketing dollars.

So, where do you start with tracking, what are those KPIs, and how do you go about keeping track of all this stuff? We will discuss call tracking, form tracking, and how you can better understand what type of return you are getting on your SEO investment. But first, let me share an important piece of advice.

Be Willing to Fail

After finishing law school, I landed a prestigious job at a big law firm in Washington, DC. On the surface, it looked perfect: great pay, talented colleagues, and plenty of professional prestige. But deep down, I knew law wasn't my passion. I was an entrepreneur at heart. I wasn't even particularly good at being a lawyer, and it certainly didn't make me happy.

It was the late '90s, and startups were everywhere. I desperately wanted in on that excitement. When my college friend Jeremy Kagan reached out in 1998 with his startup idea, EZCD—an online service that created personalized compilation CDs—I decided to take the leap. Leaving my safe, high-paying law job was scary. Moving back into my childhood bedroom felt humbling, even embarrassing.

We gave EZCD everything we had, but when Napster arrived, our business quickly collapsed. It was painful going from success and security to failure and uncertainty. Yet, surprisingly, I felt no regret. In fact, that willingness to fail and stepping away from something safe to chase something uncertain turned out to be one of the most important decisions I've ever made. It freed me to pursue a path that truly excited me, and it's a path I'm still happily following today.

Sometimes, you have to risk failure to find your real direction. And even when it doesn't work out, the leap itself can be your greatest teacher. If you're struggling to put what we've talked about into action, I challenge you to take the leap and do *something*. Don't just sit idly as the world passes you by. Show initiative. If you don't know where to begin, start with these two steps.

Step 1: Start with Google Analytics

When we talk about tracking your website traffic, the first place to start is Google Analytics. Google Analytics has been through quite a few iterations since its inception, but overall, it allows you to view data about your website and, more specifically, the traffic that is visiting your website. Google Analytics allows a webmaster to set up goals, track those goals, and see trends on their website.

To start collecting data, Google Analytics requires you to insert a piece of code in your header file on the website. You can also use Google Tag Manager to implement Google Analytics. Once the code has been on the site for a period of time, you can see the data on those website visits within the Google Analytics dashboard.

It is important to note that Google limits the amount of information it gives you about a particular searcher. For example, it is not going to give you searcher contact information; that would be absurd. However, it does give you insight into where the website visit is coming from geographically, what type of device or browser the website is being accessed from, and how long that user has stayed on your website.

One of the most valuable pieces of data that Google Analytics gives you is the source of all your website traffic. Google categorizes traffic into five separate types: organic, paid, social, referral, and direct traffic. While direct traffic is self-explanatory and refers to traffic that comes straight to your website, let's take a minute to walk through and understand each one of the other four sources.

Organic traffic comes from organic search. If you are running any sort of SEO campaign, this is the type of traffic that you want to be generating. Organic traffic originates from a money or long-tail search term. This traffic is usually the most monetizable, and if your

SEO campaign is gaining traction or is successful, this organic traffic metric should rise over time.

Paid traffic is the traffic you pay for. This is traffic that is coming from a Google Ads campaign or something of that nature. Paid traffic, as mentioned, will give you a little more detail about the searcher and the search itself. If you are running a paid Google Ads campaign, this number should rise in Google Analytics.

Social traffic refers to website visits that come to you from a social media platform. Think Instagram, Facebook, X, and LinkedIn. When you post on these platforms, and there is a link back to your website, if people click that link, that website traffic will show up in Google Analytics as referral traffic. If you are running a social media campaign, you can see if the campaign is driving traffic to your website by checking the referral traffic section of Google Analytics.

Referral traffic refers to traffic that clicks a link and comes from third-party websites. For example, if you have an Avvo listing or a scholarship campaign going, you may see Avvo or the university website in your list of referring domains in Google Analytics. Referral traffic is going to fluctuate depending on the type of campaign that you are running. For example, if you are running a banner ad campaign on a local news or radio website, you should see an uptick in referral traffic from the website you purchased the banner ad on.

Now that we know the different categories of traffic in Google Analytics, it is important to understand that not all traffic is created equally. Google Analytics gives you insight into the types of website visitors coming to your site. It reports on statistics such as engagement rate (formerly bounce rate) or how someone interacts with the page once they land on it.

As more firms experiment with AI-generated content, it's important to watch how users are engaging. If time on the site or pages per session are low, the content may not be connecting, even if the traffic looks strong.

In all of these instances, the user is visiting another page, so the pages-per-session number would be over one, and it takes time to read a page of content, so our time on site may be closer to thirty seconds or a minute. It is important to understand the nuances of your traffic so you can continue to refine and optimize your SEO campaign.

Step 2: Implement Call Tracking

Your website should have tracking phone numbers on it. I have heard all of the excuses in the book to not have call tracking on your website, but if you choose not to do so, you are committing malpractice. There may be instances where a vanity phone number is used across TV, radio, and billboards, but even then, I would recommend setting up call tracking for your website.

So what is call tracking, why do you need it, and how can you use it to better your SEO campaign? Tracking calls is not new. We used to do criminal law mailers at the firm, and at the time, we had unique tracking numbers on those fliers so we could tell which campaigns were performing and which ones were not. There are quite a few programs out there to track inbound phone calls. Two are CallRail and CallTrackingMetrics.

CallRail uses technology called dynamic number insertion to swap the phone number listed on your site with another number, depending on the source of the visit. Typically, with dynamic number insertion, a business has a pool of numbers available as people visit the website from different sources. For example, if someone is coming from an organic Google search, they will be presented with a certain number; if someone visits from Google paid ads, another number; and finally, if someone visits from Facebook, another number.

This allows you to identify the source of your calls. It is critically important for you to track all the marketing campaigns you undertake. Call tracking is one of the easiest ways for you to start to understand your true ROI on a specific marketing channel. We recommend setting up tracking numbers across all types of digital marketing campaigns. You should know how many organic calls you are receiving, how many paid calls, and how many are coming from third-party websites.

You may be wondering what happens when someone fills out a form or chats on the website instead of calling. How do you track those leads? UTM parameters are a way for you to track the source of leads. This code is added to the end of a URL and allows a business to track specific form fills or chats that come from a URL. For example, if you were running an Instagram ads campaign, and you wanted to know how many form fills you received from the campaign, you should be able to view the URLs on which the forms were filled out. If you set up the URL parameters correctly, you will know that the form fills coming from xyz.com/Instagram-ad/Utm_1 are coming from your Instagram campaign 1. By setting up UTM parameters, you can track more specific information about the traffic and its sources.

One crucial part of reporting that many businesses fall flat on is understanding a true ROI for your campaigns. If your tracking is set up well, you should be able to identify the source for all the calls, chats, and forms that are coming in through your digital campaigns. Once you have this list of leads, it is critical for you to check those leads with your customer relationship management platform (CRM) to understand if you are getting an ROI on the campaign. In other words, it is literally checking the status of each lead for every campaign.

If you see that one campaign is generating a lot of cases with low damages or folks that can't afford your services, pivot that spend to something that is more fruitful. If you see that a Google Ads campaign is converting at a high rate and the case values are higher than average, consider doubling down on Google paid and upping your spend. We refer to this as full-circle reporting, and it is crucial for comprehending your digital leads. We recommend clients do this exercise at least once a month, or every two weeks for a new campaign launch. This allows you to stay on top of campaigns and maximize the return you can get.

The goal of all lead tracking is to better understand the sources of your leads. If you are able to identify where your good leads are coming from, you can be nimble with your marketing campaigns, pivoting when things are working and pausing campaigns that are not generating a positive ROI for your business. The more data you have available to you, the more flexible you can be with your marketing dollars. This will put you and your business in the best possible position to succeed online.

Many people ask me what the main KPIs are that they should be looking at for their SEO campaign. I always go back to the main question: "What is your ROI from your SEO campaign?" This is an important question to consider. Many people think they are running good SEO campaigns if their websites are generating tens of thousands of traffic hits a month. However, as we have discussed, that traffic may not be buying traffic or healthy traffic, in which case they may not be achieving a positive ROI from their SEO campaigns.

There are other components you can consider when determining the overall success of an SEO campaign. Leads and traffic are two very important metrics for measuring SEO success. Another important metric is rankings. Without rankings, you will not get traffic or website clicks or, in turn, calls. It is important to track the keywords you want to rank for and their progress on a monthly basis. There are many tools out there that help you track organic and local rankings. Some include Ahrefs, Local Viking, Local Falcon, and Places Scout, to name a few. The key with all these tools is the setup and maintenance of the keyword list you populate in the tool. If you add content on the site targeting another keyword, be sure to add it to the tool to track its performance over time.

There is a relatively easy way to diagnose SEO problems if all your tracking is in place. Let's say that a firm's call volume has dropped significantly for truck accidents over the course of the last month. How can you figure out what is going on there? Remember: The order of rankings = traffic, and traffic = calls.

First, check your rankings for truck accident keywords. Did you lose traction organically or locally? If so, identify the page on the site that is suffering.

Check in Google Analytics to see if any truck accident pages have lost traffic over the last month. If they have, you have identified the terms and the page that needs help. Finally, you already know calls are down, so start making changes to the page that needs help. Add some content, build some links to it, and do something that will show Google you are attempting to right the ship. This simple practice is a foolproof way for you to troubleshoot any SEO problem you may be having.

Without tracking, it is extremely difficult to understand what is working and what is not working online. Firms that don't track their calls and overall campaign performances are doing themselves an extreme disservice, and I am sure they are losing out on quite a bit of campaign performance. Work with your digital marketing agency to provide the most accurate and helpful reporting for your business. Many agencies will customize their reporting to meet your needs, so work with them to figure out the best methodology for delivering this information.

Finally, be sure to act on the information. Understand your lead sources and campaign performances, where you are getting an ROI, and practice full-circle reporting. There is no telling how far these practices can take you.

Conclusion

When we started BluShark, we wanted to work with firms to help them grow and achieve their full potential. I had seen the impact firsthand of digital marketing, growing our firm from five lawyers to over seventy-five in seven states with five practice areas, all on the heels of digital. BluShark was founded on the idea that we could do this for other lawyers across the country. If we can find the right partners that embody the growth mindset that the internet was made to feed, we are destined for success.

ABOUT THE AUTHOR

An accomplished attorney and transformational thought leader, Seth Price is a founding partner and the business backbone of Price Benowitz Accident Injury Lawyers, LLP. He is also the founder and CEO of BluShark Digital, a digital marketing agency specializing in the legal sector. Seth took a two-person law firm and scaled it to more than fifty lawyers, using innovative business strategies and digital marketing tools. He leveraged the same digital expertise that helped grow his law firm to establish BluShark Digital, which has become a leading agency in its niche.

As a thought leader, Seth has become a frequent lecturer and moderator at some of the largest and most influential law conferences in the US. He speaks on a wide array of topics, focusing on how law firms can stay ahead by aligning their business development with shifting consumer habits. His talks cover a range of issues, including law firm growth, ethical considerations, best operational practices, and digital strategies. Specifically, Seth is known for his expertise in search engine optimization (SEO) and broader digital marketing strategies, both of which he integrates seamlessly into his leadership at BluShark Digital.